Reprieved at Lincoln

Reprieved at Lincoln

Lucy Ann Buxton, Emma Wade and Selina Stanhope

Malcolm Moyes

Matador
Unit E2 Airfield Business Park,
Harrison Road, Market Harborough,
Leicestershire. LE16 7UL
Tel: 0116 2792299
Email: books@troubador.co.uk
Web: www.troubador.co.uk/matador
Twitter: @matadorbooks

ISBN 978 180514 058 0

British Library Cataloguing in Publication Data.
A catalogue record for this book is available from the British Library.

Printed and bound by CPI Group (UK) Ltd, Croydon, CR0 4YY
Typeset in 12pt Minion Pro by Troubador Publishing Ltd, Leicester, UK

Matador is an imprint of Troubador Publishing Ltd

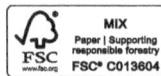

MIX
Paper | Supporting
responsible forestry
FSC
www.fsc.org
FSC® C013604

'Teach me to feel another's woe'
The Universal Prayer, **Alexander Pope, 1738**

Contents

Acknowledgements

I would like to thank the British Library which, through its digital archives of C19th and C20th newspapers, enabled me to access with relative ease the news reports and articles connected to the trials of Lucy Ann Buxton, Emma Wade and Selina Stanhope, as well as their aftermath.

I am indebted to the National Archive Collection at Kew and its helpful staff who provided me with access to the Home Office documents relating to the reprieve of Emma Wade and Selina Stanhope.

I would also like to thank the staff of the Sussex Archives for their support in accessing the diaries of George Gathorne Hardy.

My thanks are also due to the staff of Sleaford and Lincoln libraries for their invaluable support in providing access to material in their local history collections, as well as obtaining scarce out of print books through the inter-library loan system.

Finally, I would like to thank the excellent staff of the Lincolnshire Archives for their unfailing help and courtesy in enabling me access a range of useful documents in their collection.

Prologue

The lives of Lucy Ann Buxton, Emma Wade and Selina Stanhope were depressingly similar, and yet at the same time, depressingly different.

The young women in question had all been employed as domestic servants and all three had given birth to an illegitimate child: in all likelihood, they were compelled to leave domestic service, like many others in the same difficult position, on account of their unplanned 'encumbrance'.

All three were to be later put on trial for the brutal killing their own infant in quite appalling circumstances.

In each case, the verdict of the jury was that they were Guilty of wilful murder and consequently they were sentenced to death, coincidentally by the same judge, Justice Robert Lush. In all three cases, there was an immediate legal and public appeal for clemency and the women were in due course reprieved from the horrors of state execution.

At this point, the narratives of their unfortunate lives start to diverge.

Lucy Ann Buxton was found Guilty of the murder of her son, but without any further comment from the Foreman of the jury. In contrast, both Emma Wade and Selina Stanhope were found Guilty, but with a strong recommendation for mercy.

Rather than being hanged, Emma Wade, the daughter of a respectable, long-serving police constable, and brought up in the aspiring gentility of Stamford, was given a reduced sentence of one year in prison with hard labour, to be served in Lincoln. Lucy Ann Buxton, the daughter of a beer-house owner, brought up in the less sophisticated and urbane environment of Metheringham Fen and known to the authorities as a hardened petty thief, was given a reduced sentence of life imprisonment, to be served in Woking prison, Surrey, after a temporary stay in Millbank and Brixton prisons, over a hundred miles away from home. Selina Stanhope, from Langtoft, on the edge of Deeping Fen, arguably an even more remote and less salubrious location than that experienced by Lucy Ann Buxton, was also sentenced to penal servitude for life in Woking.

In 1880, Emma Wade, after having served her sentence, became a domestic servant in Market Deeping, just a few miles from Stamford; Lucy Ann Buxton almost certainly died unmourned in Woking prison, sometime between 1871 and 1881; whilst Selina Stanhope was released from the same prison in 1889, having served nine years of her sentence, to take up a position of domestic service in London.

One of the consequences of the different sentences was that Emma Wade would have had the opportunity to repair her damaged relationship with members of her family; Lucy Ann Buxton and Selina Stanhope, in all probability, never saw their family again.

There also appears to have been a similar contrast between the young women in terms of the survival of documentation relating to their divergent judicial paths. The newspapers of 1868, 1875 and 1879 respectively, reported upon the various actions of the citizens of Lincoln, Stamford and Langtoft to petition the Home Secretary for a commutation of the death sentence. The official paperwork relating to the case of Lucy Ann Buxton, which would have included a memorial requesting a reprieve, signed petitions, the trial and post-trial notes of the judge and a letter confirming the final decision of the Home Office, seems to no longer exist; and yet there are comprehensive Home Office files on Emma Wade and Selina Stanhope, consisting in both cases of well over seventy pages of documentation relating to the decision-making procedures of their reprieves.

During the mid-nineteenth century, the structure of the Home Office and its ways of working were in a state of transition, mainly as a result of external pressures from the Treasury and the findings of various parliamentary committees. Despite resistance to change rooted in the entrenched conservatism of the institution, as well as vested political and personal interests, significant progress in the evolution of the Home Office had been made by the middle of the 1870s. Driven by the reformist aspirations of the Home Secretary, Robert Lowe, during his brief tenure in the post, the Home Office became better organised and more coherent in its structures for handling criminal cases.

However, what the Home Office did not appear to become was more transparent in its decision making when it involved the Royal Prerogative of Mercy for condemned prisoners.

The broad bureaucratic structures established for the reprieve process were clear enough: memorials, petitions and pleas were submitted to the Home Office, docketed by junior and supplementary clerks, processed further by the Chief Clerk and finally forwarded to the Under-Secretary for final consideration by the Home Secretary, who was supported by his legal adviser in the more problematic cases. The evidence of the judge in the form of notes written down during the trial and a later summary of the case, sometimes including additional evidence not considered in court or which might have heightened existing doubts, were also included with these documents.

The final outcome of the bureaucratic process of discussion and evaluation of a capital case was a bland formulaic letter from the Under-Secretary of State for the Home Department confirming the decision, sent to the Governor of the gaol where the prisoner was being held, the organisers of the memorials and other interested parties, but without any explanation of how the decision was reached and therefore lacking any meaningful accountability. Once filed away, the paper trail which had determined the life or death of an individual, disappeared from view for a hundred years, sometimes more, thus contributing further to a sense of secrecy and a lack of openness surrounding decision making at the Home Office.

The sections of the *Report of the Capital Punishment Commission*, published in 1866, which minuted questions and responses concerning the exercise of the Royal Prerogative, not only suggest that there was a lack of transparency at the Home Office, but also a carefully constructed culture of institutional concealment, dressed up as impeccable discretion. When pressed on key issues of openness, the Home Secretary at the time, Spencer Horace Walpole, provided answers which were slippery, ambiguous and, at times, blatantly evasive.

When questioned by the Oxford academic

and Liberal MP, Charles Neate, about the alleged existence of a Minute in the Home Office which recorded the grounds for every reprieve, he was less than candid. Unhelpfully, he referred his questioner to the published judicial statistics 'which will inform anybody who takes an interest in the subject what were the facts upon which commutation was granted'. Pressed as to whether or not there was a fuller Minute kept at the Home Office, the smoke and mirrors of political evasion continued: 'All papers are kept', he reassured the assembled Commissioners. In one final attempt to pin down the Home Secretary on the issue, Neate asked the Right Honourable Spencer Horace Walpole, if the signature of the Secretary of State for the Home Office appeared on the papers to which he referred. 'His decision is usually noted on the back of them', was the conveniently vague retort.

Replying to the question of Dr Stephen Lushington, Judge of the High Court of the Admiralty, concerning the possibility of greater openness and transparency at the Home Office, it is not surprising that the Home Secretary thought that both the sharing and the free flow of information on the subject of reprieves from the death sentence would lead to very great mischief: the general public was clearly not to be trusted with such knowledge.

What he meant by 'mischief' was defined more precisely when grilled by Neate on the subject of whether the public should, as a matter of course, be informed of the reasons for a decision to reprieve or not reprieve. His forthright opinion was that such transparency about the judgment of the Home Secretary would inevitably lead to a very unsatisfactory situation of 'everybody questioning it as if it was a court of appeal', as opposed to a court of mercy.

Despite procedural changes at the Home Office during the following years, sharing the reasons for a final decision on the exercise of the Royal Prerogative by the Home Secretary was clearly not going to be one of them. The acerbic comment from Lincolnshire born Lord Vere Henry Hobart that the reprieve process amounted to little more than 'a secret trial' captured the sense of dismay and dissatisfaction with the culture of concealment at the Home Office, albeit from the less representative perspective of the undermining of public confidence in the law by overturning a death sentence.

The accounts of the progress of a reprieve appeal in the popular press were predictable in view of their lack of direct access to what was urgently taking place behind closed doors in Whitehall. Some were bland and sober narratives of the worthy efforts of influential individuals to organise a memorial on behalf of 'the unfortunate prisoner', and to gather local support for his or her reprieve. Others used the sensational story of a death sentence and a possible last minute reprieve to question the morality of capital punishment, the coherence of the criminal law on murder, the supposed deterrent effect of the extreme penalty of the law, and sometimes all three.

However, despite the growing confidence of the popular press, with its more robust sense of entitlement to comment directly upon issues of current interest and to consequently shape public opinion, none were in a position to produce a definitive account of how the process of reprieve had unfolded for Lucy Ann Buxton, Emma Wade and Selina Stanhope, sitting in the bleak bareness of the condemned cell in Lincoln, waiting to hear either the best or the worst of news.

Occasionally, and after the fact of a reprieve, the newspapers celebrated the success of a life being spared by way of the unctuous fiction of Royal Mercy, although in some cases, they were careful to point out that they did not necessarily endorse the abolition of hanging. Also after the fact, credit for the happy outcome was sometimes attributed to the influence of particular individuals, rather than to the supposed gracious intervention of her Majesty - men of power and social standing, who had a more direct and effective access to the Home Office than that offered by the submission of letters and petitions.

Such accounts are not inaccurate, but are only

partially true, based upon the limited material made available to the press for public consumption. The letters of Sir John Dalrymple Hay, MP for Stamford, and Edward Chaplin, MP for Lincoln, for example, which appeared in the press and which chronicled their part in the reprieve of Emma Wade and Selina Stanhope respectively, provided interesting information for the reader to reflect upon, but left large gaps in the narrative.

Both men quite clearly had face to face conversations with the Home Secretary on the subject of the reprieve, but the newspapers made no comment on issues which might arise from such private meetings, not least the contradiction of the Home Secretary's own unwritten rule that he did not discuss criminal cases with individuals.

A similar disparity is evident in the reported response to Edward Chaplin's request to the Home Secretary that the draconian life sentence meted out to Selina Stanhope be reduced. His assertion that 'there was an invariable rule that he had never remembered to have departed from, that in the case of the sentence of death being respited it was always penal servitude for life' was a somewhat surprising lapse of memory in that Emma Wade had been sentenced on his watch to one year in prison only four years earlier.

According to the further testimony of Walpole, there were procedural rules which the Home

Secretary followed, but these seemed to have a useful flexibility about them.

In response to questions from Thomas O'Hagan, Attorney General of Ireland, concerning the perception that the Home Secretary invariably followed the advice of the trial judge in cases of mitigation and as to whether there was a fixed rule concerning any possible disagreement, Walpole was clear and confident in his responses: 'I believe that the Home Office has always followed the recommendation of the Judge, as respects a mitigation of the sentence'. On the other hand, he was equally clear and confident that the judge's opinion was not always followed: 'I myself in one case acted contrary to the recommendation of the Judge'.

The issue of whether the trial judge's report was decisive and so amounted to a procedural rule was further probed by the persistently inquisitive Mr Neate.

Approaching the question less directly, he asked Walpole, 'is it not very unusual for the Home Secretary to act at variance with the recommendation of the judge who tried the case'? The Home Secretary seemed to agree with Charles Neale that it was not usual to disagree with the trial judge, quite simply because in his experience there was 'no necessity to differ from the Judge'. However, the 'no necessity' of one sentence then became a 'now and then necessity' in the next: in such a circumstance the Secretary of State took upon himself the responsibility of differing.

At this point, Neate took a more blunt approach, asking Walpole whether or not it was 'a settled rule' at the Home Office that the Secretary of State would not 'act at variance with the recommendation of the judge'? The response of the Home Secretary, for once, was unequivocal: 'Certainly not'.

Spencer Horace Walpole seemed to be warming to the task of using unqualified brisk assertions when he responded to Mr Neate's follow-up question. Asked if the judgment of the Home Secretary was therefore 'entirely unfettered', he was once again very clear: 'Absolutely unfettered'. Just for the record and to ensure total clarity, Mr Neate asked Secretary Walpole if his decisions were based solely on his 'judgement and conscience' could he assume that they were absolutely unfettered? Strictly speaking, the reply which assured his interrogator that he 'may take it that everything which is done by the Secretary of State, in revising the punishment, is done entirely upon his own responsibility', was not a direct answer to the terms of the question. It may be that Mr Walpole, at this point, sensed that he had been speaking a little too openly and honestly in his responses to Charles Neate and so added as a qualification, despite his earlier claim of being 'absolutely unfettered', that he always acted 'with all the aid he can get'. It was perhaps not so much an abdication of ultimate responsibility as a nervous awareness of the nascent intrusions of the press into the murky business of politics and also a deep mistrust of mischievous public opinion. Responsibility for the decision to allow another human being to live or die was indeed an awesome one, but one perhaps best shared, especially if it turned out to be unpopular or even wrong.

In the course of being questioned, the Home Secretary exercised, for the most part, a skilled politician's caution in avoiding unqualified, direct answers. The most interesting exception to this obfuscation and guarded avoidance, again in response to Charles Neale, was an assertion which would have been impossible to defend had it been pressed further. Walpole was asked whether in the course of reviewing a capital case the Home Secretary went into the evidence of the trial? Perhaps worn down by the annoying persistence of Mr Neale, the response was as frank as it may have been peeved: 'Every atom of it', the Home Secretary insisted.

That the Home Secretary, by his own earlier admission, relied on the notes and report of the trial judge, completely contradicted his large claim to have had such a detailed knowledge of all the evidence heard at the trial. An examination of the documents supplied by Robert Lush to the Home Secretary of the time make it obvious that his account of the evidence was inevitably selective, incomplete and therefore partial – gaps which some petitioners perhaps hoped to fill by submitting newspaper trial reports to the Home Office in their support for a reprieve.

Chapter One

Lucy Ann Buxton (1844-?)

Lucy Ann Buxton: Timeline

6th September, 1844: Lucy Ann Buxton, daughter of Ann and Thomas Buxton, grocer and keeper of a beer house, in Metheringham Fen, baptised.

14th April, 1851: Ann Buxton, mother of Lucy Ann Buxton, charged at the Lincoln City Sessions, found guilty and sentenced to eight months in Lincoln prison for the theft of wearing apparel, having already served four months during the postponement of her trial, due to ill-health.

5th April, 1854: Ann Buxton, aged fifty, buried in Metheringham.

10th April, 1854: inquest into the death of Ann Buxton: inconclusive verdict.

1860: birth of Thomas Frederick Buxton, illegitimate son of Lucy Ann Buxton.

18th August, 1866: Lucy Ann Buxton found guilty of stealing a watch in Leeds and summarily sentenced to two months in prison.

12th October, 1867: Lucy Ann Buxton sentenced to six months in Lincoln prison, with hard labour, for stealing wearing apparel and other valuables from the home of her former employer.

December, 1867: birth of John Edward Buxton, illegitimate son of Lucy Ann Buxton, in Lincoln prison.

11th April, 1868: Lucy Ann Buxton released from Lincoln prison, who goes to live with her father, Thomas Buxton, in Metheringham Fen.

24th April, 1868: sudden death of John Edward Buxton.

27th April, 1868: inquest into the death of John Edward Buxton at the Windmill public house, Metheringham. Lucy Ann Buxton taken into police custody.

28th April, 1868: Lucy Ann Buxton brought before magistrate, John Bromhead, on the charge of child murder and remanded until the 5th May.

29th April, 1868: burial of John Edward Buxton in Metheringham, aged four and a half months.

4th May, 1868: Lucy Ann Buxton brought before

the magistrate, Reverend G F Apthorp, and remanded for a further week. She escapes from Kesteven Police Station during the evening.

5th May, 1868: Lucy Ann Buxton rearrested in Bardney and sent to the Kirton in Lindsey lock-up.

9th May, 1868: Lucy Ann Buxton received into Lincoln Castle prison, on remand, suspected of child murder.

11th May, 1868: resumed inquest into the death of John Edward Buxton: coroner's jury finds Lucy Ann Buxton guilty of child murder and she is sent for trial at the next session of the Lincoln Assizes.

24th July, 1868: trial of Lucy Ann Buxton at the Lincoln Assizes for the wilful murder of her infant son and found guilty: sentenced to death by Justice Robert Lush. Taken back to Lincoln Castle prison to await her execution.

27th July, 1868: Lucy Ann Buxton informed of her execution date of Friday, 7th August, due to take place at noon.

4th August, 1868: letter from the Home Office sent to James Foster, Governor of Lincoln Castle prison, commuting Lucy Ann Buxton's death sentence to penal servitude for life.

23rd September, 1868: Lucy Ann Buxton received into Millbank prison from Lincoln Castle.

13th March, 1869: removed from Millbank prison and taken to Brixton prison.

17th December, 1869: removed from Brixton prison and returned to Millbank prison.

10th June, 1870: removed from Millbank prison and taken to Woking prison.

2nd April, 1871: Lucy Ann Buxton recorded in 1871 Census as a prisoner at Woking prison.

'Dark Domestic History': the condemnation and reprieve of Lucy Ann Buxton

At the time of the arrest of Lucy Ann Buxton for the suspected murder of her infant son, on the 27th April, 1868, the family was well-established and well-known in the Tan Vats area of Metheringham Fen.

On 10th December, 1828, Thomas Buxton, a thirty-two year old widower, born in Blankney Fen, married twenty-four year old Ann Marshall, also of Blankney Fen. His first wife, Sarah Whittaker, whom he had married on the 1st June, 1820, had died on the 22nd March, 1827, aged thirty-two. Both marriages took place in Metheringham.

In 1841, the Buxton household, living in Tan Vats, Metheringham Fen, on the day of the Census, consisted of:

Thomas Buxton, aged 45, cottager

Ann Buxton, aged 35

Mary Buxton, aged 14

Lucy Buxton, aged 9

Ann Buxton, aged 7

Maria Buxton, aged 3

Sarah Buxton, aged 1

In 1851, the Buxton household, still living in Tan

Vats, Metheringham Fen, on the day of the Census consisted of:

> Thomas Buxton, married, aged 55, born in
>   Blankney Fen
> Jane Buxton, daughter, aged 11, born in
>   Metheringham
> Thomas Buxton, son, aged 9 , born in
>   Metheringham
> Joseph Buxton, son, aged 6, born in
>   Metheringham
> Lucy Buxton, daughter, aged 4, born in
>   Metheringham

In 1861, the Buxton household, located specifically at the White Swan Inn, in Tan Vats, on the day of the Census, consisted of:

> Thomas Buxton, widower, aged 65, publican and
>   agricultural labourer, born in Blankney Fen
> Jane Buxton, unmarried, aged 21, born in
>   Metheringham
> Thomas Buxton, grandson, aged 10 months, born
>   in Lincoln
> Mary Abbot, house servant, aged 52, born in
>   Metheringham

White's *Directory* for 1842 lists Thomas Buxton as

a grocer in Tan Vats and in 1856 as the keeper of a beer house in the same place. The various baptismal records of his children record him as a grocer (1829); a tradesman (1833 and 1834) and a publican (1838).

Thomas Buxton was buried in Metheringham in 1870, having spent, it appears, his entire life within the tightly circumscribed areas of Blankney and Metheringham Fens.

Even allowing for absence on the day, the most cursory glance at the Census data suggests unfortunate and sometimes puzzling change over time in the Buxton household, rather than steady continuity. Of the five young children listed in the 1841 Census, two died before the next Census was taken: Ann(e) Buxton died on the 1st March, 1842, aged seven years, and Lucy Buxton died in the second quarter of 1844, aged twelve years.

In the 1851 Census, Thomas Buxton is recorded as being married with four children, three of whom are additions to the family from the previous Census, including Lucy Ann; the only child who also appeared in the 1841 Census is Sarah Buxton, baptised Sarah Jane Buxton, who confusingly appears in the later Census as Jane Buxton.

The very obvious omission from the 1851 Census is the wife of Thomas Buxton, Ann Buxton, with whom he had eight or more children.

The realities beneath and behind the silent

data fragment relating to Ann Buxton reveal an uncomfortable story which the popular press did much to publicise and, in due course, use as part of an extended narrative tenuously linked to the alleged poisoning of an infant by its mother, Lucy Ann Buxton.

On the 10th January, 1851, both the *Lincolnshire Chronicle* and the *Stamford Mercury* reported on the crime of 'extensive shop-lifting' which had taken place on the premises of John Norton, draper, located in St Peter at Arches, Lincoln, which had been discovered in late December of the previous year. The adjective 'extensive' used by the *Lincolnshire Chronicle* to describe the thefts was no exaggeration. The full haul consisted of twenty-six yards of blue silk, twelve and a half yards of black silk, three silk handkerchiefs, five other silk handkerchiefs, a black silk handkerchief, a shawl, six yards of ribbon, five yards of Cobourg silk and a boa.

The trial of Ann Buxton of Tan Vats, Metheringham, aged forty-six, accused of the multiple thefts, took place in front of Recorder N R Clarke on the 9th January, at the Lincoln City Sessions, but was soon adjourned. A true bill had been found against her, but the trial was unable to proceed as the court had received a medical certificate stating that the accused was too ill to be brought up for trial. The case was therefore ordered to be postponed until the following Session in April.

According to both newspapers, the accused was 'a notorious opium-eater' who, being deprived of the narcotic in prison, had become unfit to stand trial, having been ill in bed since the 2ⁿᵈ January. The *Lincolnshire Chronicle*'s description of Ann Buxton's indisposition was rather more dramatic than that of the *Stamford Mercury*: she was not so much ill, as 'completely prostrated'.

The resumed trial on the 14ᵗʰ April, again before the Recorder, Mr N R Clarke, resulting in the conviction of Mrs Buxton, was reported with a great deal of interest by the *Lincolnshire Chronicle* and the *Stamford Mercury* on the 18ᵗʰ April.

The main focus of the evidence was upon the disappearance from John Norton's shop of the twenty-six yards of blue silk, although he had been aware that other goods had been disappearing 'in a manner that could not be accounted for'. Mrs Buxton, it emerged, was well known to John Norton, as she was a regular visitor to the shop on market days and so she had become a trusted customer.

The misplaced trust of Mr Norton came to light after Ann Buxton gave a sample of the blue silk to a local hawker, Robert McGuire, on 31ˢᵗ December, 1850, who had taken it to Thomas Axtall, a Lincoln tailor, to get his considered opinion of its value. Unfortunately for Mrs Buxton, the daughter of the tailor had recently tried to buy some of the same blue silk from Norton's shop, but had been told that there was none in stock. The suspicions of Thomas Axtall having been aroused, a warrant to search the premises of the house of Ann Buxton was issued to Police Superintendent Thomas Ashton. The blue silk was discovered in an upstairs drawer, along with the other stolen items, some of which had been 'secreted under paper'.

Confronted by the discovery of the blue silk, Ann Buxton claimed that 'she had taken it by mistake and intended to return it the following Friday'. Henry Draycott, the shop assistant to John Norton, however, was not only able to identify the missing blue silk, but also 'spoke to the other articles as being like in kind and quality to the goods missed from the shop at different times'.

In his summary of the case, the Recorder pointed out the obvious inconsistency of trying to sell the blue silk to a hawker whilst claiming that she intended to return it: the Petit Jury agreed and found Mrs Buxton guilty of robbery. In passing sentence, he also made it clear that she had only escaped transportation because it was her first offence. Consequently, he sentenced her to prison for eight more months, as she had already been imprisoned for four months, prior to the trial.

In the accounts of the trial, the newspapers made it clear that Thomas Buxton was not aware of his wife's criminal activities: according to the *Lincolnshire Chronicle*, he was 'a respectable beer-shop keeper', and in the view of the *Stamford Mercury*, he was he was 'a very respectable cottager'.

The incarceration of Ann Buxton was not the final fragment of her life to play out in the media.

On Wednesday, 5th April, 1854, she was buried in Metheringham, aged fifty years. On the following Monday, an inquest was held in front of the coroner, James Hitchins, to establish the cause of death. The report in the *Stamford Mercury* for that week recorded the evidence of Thomas Buxton, who told the court that his wife had complained of pains in her head at about 5 o'clock on the Saturday evening, and at around 9 o'clock, whilst sitting in her room, she became drowsy and fell asleep. Once in her bed, she became insensible and remained so until morning, when she died. The jury returned the unhelpful verdict that Ann Buxton had died after being in a state of insensibility for some hours, 'but from what cause that insensibility was occasioned the evidence was not sufficient to show'.

There was no reference to opium addiction.

The 1851 Census records that Lucy (Ann) Buxton, aged four, was living with her father in Metheringham Fen. Ten years later, logically aged fourteen, but in reality aged seventeen, if the *Metheringham Baptismal Register* is correct, her name does not appear.

However, the 1861 Census does list a grandson, also named Thomas Buxton, aged ten months, who was almost certainly the illegitimate son of Lucy Ann Buxton.

The whereabouts of Lucy Ann Buxton at this time, and to some extent afterwards, is rather elusive. What is clear, however, is that in August 1866 she was caught stealing a watch in Leeds, for which she was summarily given a two month prison sentence, and that in October, 1867, she was tried in Lincoln for the theft of a quantity of 'wearing apparel' from the house of her former employer, and given six months in prison with hard labour.

It was a depressing story of a downward spiral into crime which was tracked by the Lincolnshire newspapers with a mixture of regret and censure.

Lucy Ann Buxton appeared before Mr W Rudgard and Mr J R Battle on Monday, 23rd September, charged with the theft of property during the evening of the 21st September, which was valued at £8. The haul included a black silk jacket, one checked silk dress, one white tablecloth, one nightdress, one pair of stays and five silver spoons.

After being remanded for a week, her case was heard in front of Mr J R Battle and Mr H Harvey, on Monday 30th September, and was reported in full by the *Lincolnshire Chronicle* on the 4th October. It was the second time that the paths of John Richard Battle and Lucy Ann Buxton had crossed in a short period, and it was not to be the last.

The robbery from the house of Lincoln butcher, George Hardy, situated in Magpies Square, on the High Street, would have been read with either incredulity at its comic ineptness or outrage at its brazen contempt for the concept of private ownership. On the one hand, Lucy Ann allowed the two key witnesses living in the house to witness her in plain sight and, on the other, she calmly helped herself to various valuables, mainly owned by the wife of Mr Hardy and carried them off a short distance to a lodging house adjacent to the Robin Hood public house on Sincil Street, where she was lodging.

The main witness to the crime was Elizabeth Ann Bosworth, the servant of George Hardy, who had been disturbed at 9 o'clock in the evening by a knock on the door: at the threshold, she had encountered Lucy Ann Buxton, who politely enquired whether or not she was at the residence of George Hardy, as she had a message to deliver from Mrs Hardy. She told Miss Bosworth that her mistress, as a matter of some urgency, wished her to go to Mr Hardy's shop with a basket, whilst Lucy Ann minded the house during her absence. After lighting the gas and inviting the helpful messenger to take a seat, the obedient, but rather naïve servant girl departed, leaving Lucy Ann Buxton in charge of an eleven year old boy, Thomas Hardy, as well as the contents of the house.

The accused did not waste any time and immediately ascertained the whereabouts of candles to enable her to safely climb the stairs. The young boy deposed that he saw his new carer go upstairs, but he did not see her come down; indeed, he did not see her again that night. Not surprisingly, on discovering that Mrs Hardy had not really sent for her, Elizabeth Bosworth rushed back to the house; it was equally unsurprising that there was no sign of the house-minder.

After the discovery of the theft was reported by Mr Hardy, Police Detective William Lilburn took a detailed description of the mystery messenger, and at around 6 o'clock on the Sunday evening he tracked her down on Newland Street West, where she was arrested and taken to the police station. Following Detective Lilburn's impressive rapid result, the suspect was identified by Elizabeth Bosworth and young Thomas Hardy as the woman who had been at the house the night before. The response of Lucy Ann was to claim that she had only arrived in the city at 1.30 that day.

The scepticism of the detective concerning her story was justified when he visited the lodging house on Sincil Street and discovered a black velvet mantle, a silk dress, six silver spoons, five plated silver spoons, a table cloth, a plated sauce ladle, a night dress, a pair of stays, a muslin jacket and a quantity of calico, all of which were identified by Mr Hardy as his property.

On the following morning, Detective Lilburn asked Lucy Ann where she had acquired the goods and she admitted that they were from the house of her former employer, George Hardy.

After Mr Hardy identified under oath the articles found by the detective, John Bailey, a warder from Leeds City prison, produced a certificate from the Clerk of the Peace for Leeds which confirmed that Lucy Ann Buxton had been imprisoned for two months for a felony committed in 1866.

The prisoner offered no defence and was committed for trial at the next Quarter Sessions.

The trial was reported in the *Lincolnshire Chronicle* and the *Stamford Mercury* on the 18th October; perhaps because there was so little to contend, the foregone conclusion of a prison sentence was briefly described in one paragraph by both newspapers.

Appearing in front of the Honourable Gowran Charles Vernon, on the 12th October, Lucy Ann Buxton, pleaded guilty to the case presented against her, and she was sentenced to six months in Lincoln prison.

The barest of narrative bones describing the judicial process might have been given a more human profile had the newspaper been given access to a letter dated 18th October, written in a beautiful cursive script which was in strange contrast to the mangled spelling, punctuation and grammar of the contents. It had been sent to the court by Thomas Buxton, the stressed and bewildered father of Lucy Ann, and requested clemency for his daughter:

> *Sir*
>
> *I ham sorry to have to rite to you gentlemen in respect of my Daughter Lucy Ann Buxton which she as Don very rong for what I hear that I hope that you will be Merceful as you can I ham so uneasy that I carnt com to see her at present She has always ad a good Home and a good Father and wot she can don it for The Lord only knows.*
>
> *I Remain*
> *Yours Thos.Buxton*

Inquest into the death of John Edward Buxton at The Windmill Public House, Metheringham, in front of Dr George Mitchinson, Monday 27th April, 1868

The formal inquest into the premature death of John Edward Buxton, aged four and a half months, was reported by both the *Stamford Mercury* and the *Lincolnshire Chronicle* on 1st May. Despite an inquest being an objective investigation into an unexplained death, it is clear that the two newspapers had their own preferred agenda of wilful murder: the *Stamford Mercury* caught the attention of its readers with the headline, 'Suspected Child Murder', whilst the *Lincolnshire Chronicle* chose to draw attention to the location of the crime with the caption, 'Suspected Murder in Metheringham'.

Of the two newspapers, the *Stamford Mercury* was the more restrained in its reporting, although both had no doubt that Lucy Ann Buxton, the mother of the dead infant, was guilty of administering poison. Both were equally clear that the criminal record of the young woman, which had not formed any part of the inquest procedure, was relevant to an understanding of the case.

The *Lincolnshire Chronicle* started by reminding its readers of a report which had appeared in their columns 'some months ago' relating to the theft of wearing apparel and other articles by her from the house of George Hardy, her former employer, for which Lucy Ann Buxton had been found guilty and imprisoned in the city's gaol for six months.

The newspaper was now able to continue the sorry story of the unfortunate young woman, based upon material culled from the small number of inquest witnesses. The narrative was constructed from the point at which Lucy Ann Buxton, accidentally and ironically renamed Brixton, completed her sentence and returned to the house of her father in Metheringham on 11th April. By way of additional useful background information, it was noted that Mr Buxton kept a beer house in Metheringham; but in order to reassure any concerned reader, the report also noted that Mr Buxton was 'said to be a respectable man'.

On 23rd April, Lucy Ann Buxton went to visit her brother's house, also in Metheringham, taking her infant child with her. The following day, she accompanied her sister-in-law, Mary Buxton, across some fields to fetch some milk and butter, but had to turn back as the child was crying and 'became convulsed'. She did not, however, return to her brother's house, but instead went to the cottage of a neighbour, Mrs Lacey, to get her advice as to what to do. Mrs Lacey, not surprisingly, suggested that she took her son to see a doctor.

She waited for her sister-in-law to return from across the fields, whom she then asked to go with her to see Dr Bower: but before reaching the house of the Metheringham surgeon, they discovered that he was not at home. At which point, a Mrs Boldock, who lived close by, invited both women into her cottage to await the doctor's return. After a short time, Lucy Ann Buxton, decided to go by herself to the doctor's house to find out when he was likely to return, and was told 1 o'clock.

On returning to Mrs Boldock's house, she asked her sister-in-law to go and fetch Thomas Hayland, a retired surgeon also living in Metheringham, but before his eventual arrival the infant had died.

The details of the train of events were supplemented by several short witness statements made in front of the coroner. Mrs Boldock confirmed that she has seen the child 'much convulsed' and was in no doubt that it had died in a convulsive fit. Dr Bower subsequently examined the dead child, observing that its hands were clenched, leading him to also suggest that it had died from convulsions.

At this point in the proceedings, at the suggestion of one of the jurymen, the coroner asked Mary Buxton whether her father had kept any poison in the house – specifically *Battle's Vermin Killer*. Mary Buxton, according to the newspaper, said that her father had admitted owning some and it had gone missing. Further, she told the inquest that only her sister-in-law, Lucy Ann Buxton, could have had access to it.

This seemed to have been a tipping point as Dr Mitchinson adjourned the enquiry until a post mortem examination of the child could be made.

The report, inaccurate in some of its details, ended with a rapid résumé of what followed. The contents of the stomach of the dead infant were sent off to London for Professor Alfred Swaine Taylor to analyse. Lucy Ann Buxton (still insistently Brixton) was taken into custody by the police and the next day was brought before the magistrate, John Bromhead, on suspicion of child murder. She was remanded until the following Tuesday, by which time it was hoped that the expert opinion of Professor Taylor would be available.

The *Stamford Mercury* reported the case similarly, although without labouring the story of Lucy Ann Buxton's conviction for theft. It did, however, draw attention to a significant detail in quite different terms which related to *Battle's Vermin Killer*. According to the Lincoln newspaper's version of Mary Buxton's deposition, the owner of the poison was Thomas Buxton, the father of Lucy Ann; the Stamford newspaper, however, reported that the poison was in the house of her brother, the husband of Mary Buxton. The extended testimony of Mary Buxton at the resumed inquest was to later confirm that this had been the case.

The Stamford paper's report differed from the *Lincolnshire Chronicle* further by noting that Lucy Ann Buxton was brought up in front of the Reverend G F Apthorp, rather than John Bromhead: it may be, of course, that both were serving on the Bench at the time.

The much anticipated findings of Professor Taylor, scheduled to be heard on Monday, 3rd May, the intended date for the resumption of the adjourned inquest, were unfortunately delayed. However, for the readers of the *Lincolnshire Chronicle*, disappointment was to be replaced by unanticipated excitement and possible astonishment. On the evening of 8th May, the newspaper reported that Lucy Ann Buxton, suspected child poisoner, held on remand at Kesteven Police Station, had managed to escape.

The account of the incident was sympathetic to the officer in charge at the time, but found it difficult to convincingly explain away the ease with which the prisoner managed to unlock a door and then clamber out of a window without being noticed. It appears that Superintendent John Allingham, the man in charge of the station, which was also his home, checked on Lucy Ann at 7 o'clock that evening, in order to allow her to exercise in the yard. At some point, either before or after exercise, she complained to the officer that she was unwell and that her feet were very cold. The kindly superintendent allowed her to sit in the kitchen in front of the fire in order to revive.

Shortly before having to leave the station, his kindness, or his gullibility, allowed the prisoner to take some sewing upstairs and sit with his wife, who was confined to her room at the time. According to his own account, he carefully locked all the doors and gave the keys to a nurse and it was at this point he discovered that the prisoner was missing, having simply unlocked the door of the front room - the only door in which a key was left - and had resourcefully made her exit via a window.

Despite an immediate alert and a thorough scouring of the immediate area in the dark by several police constables, no trace was found of the fugitive from justice.

Having received information the next morning concerning the whereabouts of Lucy Ann Buxton, an officer was dispatched to Bardney to apprehend her at the house of Mrs Hird, a relative, although the newspaper was to later correct this to the house of a Mr Morris. She was then taken to the Kirton in Lindsey lock-up which was presumably more secure than Kesteven Police Station.

Resumed inquest into the death of John Edward Buxton at The Windmill Public House, Metheringham, in front of Dr George Mitchinson, Monday 27th April, 1868

The *Lincolnshire Chronicle*'s report on the resumed inquest, published on 15th May, was extensive and detailed, reporting the depositions of all the witnesses, including the chemical analysis of the stomach and viscera of the dead infant by Professor Swaine Taylor. The headline, 'Metheringham Poisoning Case. Committal of the Accused' made it clear to the reader that Lucy Ann Buxton would soon be on trial for her life in Lincoln.

The first deposition to be heard was that of Mary

Buxton, whose account at the adjourned inquest had provided the fundamental narrative of what had taken place on April 24th. This latest account from Mrs Buxton was much more precise, in particular in its information about the condition of the infant the day before its death and during his final hours of life, as well as what it had eaten and drank during the course of 23rd and 24th April.

Lucy Ann Buxton had visited her house on Thursday, 23rd April, at around noon, accompanied by her child, and also by Mary Abbot, the elderly housekeeper of her father-in-law. They had dinner together and Mary Buxton took the child from its mother's arms, undressed and nursed it for some time. The child had been fed with bread and water before dinner, which Lucy Ann Buxton had retrieved from the dairy and had prepared herself.

The infant appeared to be in good health at this point and was nursed for most of the afternoon by Mrs Buxton, before he was put to bed.

The account of the remainder of the afternoon was an unexceptional one of Lucy Ann Buxton breastfeeding her son, Mary Abbot nursing the child whilst the mother went out into the fields to gather primroses and finally, after tea, Mary Buxton and Mary Abbot taking a pleasant evening walk back to the house of Thomas Buxton in Metheringham Fen.

Mary Buxton pointed out that they were not

accompanied by Lucy Ann Buxton who was left alone in the house for around twenty minutes.

She had returned home at 7 o'clock that evening, handed the infant back to its mother, who fed him with more bread and water, before putting the child to bed. Mary Buxton did not see any more of the child until 6 o'clock the next morning: at this point, she insisted, it 'seemed quite well'.

The timeline of the next day's events was closely defined: at 7 o'clock in the morning, Lucy Ann Buxton gave her infant son more food and breast fed him; at half-past eight, they went together to Mr Greenham's to buy some milk.

Mary Buxton then interrupted her narrative to make it clear to the coroner's court that from the time that John Edward Buxton entered her house on the Thursday to the time that the infant was taken away on the Friday, she did not prepare any of his food.

The continuation of the narrative differed slightly from the version of the events reported earlier by the newspaper, mainly in terms of its lack of drama concerning Lucy Ann Buxton's decision to turn back on the journey undertaken with her sister-in-law to buy milk.

Mary Buxton was very precise that she had turned back 'within one field of Mr Greenham's foreman's house'. There was no mention of the child being in any distress at the time: she simply handed over the infant to his mother who headed back to the house. The child had not been crying or convulsing as the *Lincolnshire Chronicle* had earlier reported, but quite the opposite: the little boy had been quiet and asleep during their walk.

The next time she saw the child was at Mrs Lacey's house, sometime between 10 and 11 o'clock that morning. He was seated on Lucy Ann Buxton's knee and was convulsing badly. What followed was a graphic description of the distressing symptoms of strychnine poisoning. The hands were clenched and the eyes were turned upwards; its whole body 'appeared stiff and all in a piece'. The child continued to have convulsive fits, punctuated by the occasional respite when it became less stiff, what Mrs Buxton called 'limber', and whined pitifully. His eyes 'were bolder, staring whilst it was in a fit'; when the convulsions returned after any brief respite, 'it gave a jump and became quite stiff'.

The two women left the house of Mrs Lacey with the child in order to get medical attention from the local surgeon, Dr Bower. Mrs Buxton carried the infant who continued to suffer from convulsions. In a variant version of events to that reported from the initial inquest, Mary Buxton said that at about 11 o'clock she handed over the child to her sister-in-law who she understood 'was going to take it to Mr Bower's'.

She saw the child about two minutes later at the house of Mrs Boldock, who lived quite close to the doctor. He was still in convulsions when she took him from Lucy Ann, who went to try and get information about the intended return of Dr Bower. After a time, Mrs Buxton went to find Dr Hayland for help, whom she told about the condition of the child. On returning to the house of Mrs Boldock, she discovered that the child had died, at around 12 noon. Possibly in response to a question from the coroner, Mrs Buxton explained that the reason for Dr Hayland not having been called out sooner was that she had earlier seen him going out of Metheringham, as she and her sister-in-law had come into the village.

Other than the unexplained return to the house by Lucy Ann Buxton, the deposition of Mary Buxton so far had offered little important new evidence to support any suspicion of foul play. What followed, however, made a significant contribution to building a case against her, in that it related to *Battle's Vermin Killer*, the deadly poison briefly mentioned in passing towards the end of the initial inquest.

Battle's Vermin Killer, which contained three-quarters of a grain of strychnine in every three pence packet, was available over the counter or through the post, and was a popular solution to deal with domestic and farm vermin. According to the numerous adverts of the time, the product 'never fails to give satisfaction', as 'mice appear attracted to it as by magic, eat it readily, tumble over, and die on the spot'.

Unfortunately, it was also a popular solution for people wishing to end their lives: numerous investigations into Lincolnshire suicides, between 1860 and 1871, identified *Battle's Vermin Killer* as the ultimate cause of the self-destruction. Perhaps even worse, as far as Lucy Ann Buxton was concerned, it was also identified as the poison used in the sensational case of Elizabeth Vamplew of Grimoldby, the thirteen year-old girl accused of killing an infant in her care in 1862, and who was subsequently found guilty of manslaughter and sentenced to twelve years in prison, eventually ending up at Parkhurst, on the Isle of Wight.

Mary Buxton continued her deposition by confirming that on the 23rd April, the day when she was visited by her sister-in-law, she had mouse powder in a packet 'similar to the one now produced': at the time, it was in the dairy between the shelf and the glasses. She had purchased it from the shop of Mr Thompson and had paid three pence for it. She had probably only used about half of the packet.

On the following day, prompted by something her father-in-law had said, she went to look for the mouse powder, but despite her best efforts she could not find it anywhere in the house. On the same day, around noon, she was re-making her kitchen fire, which had gone out, and she discovered a piece of yellow paper with printing upon it, amongst the cinders.

On returning home after the death of the infant, she had found her house door locked, but was able to let herself in as she had a key. She discovered that in her absence a saucepan had been used, as it was not in its usual place. It was usually kept in the stable for the purpose of wetting corn. She had also discovered two eggs on the table.

The information about the saucepan and the eggs, as reported, seemed inconsequential, but her parting words from the witness stand were a good deal more important. According to Mrs Buxton, she was visited on Saturday, 25th April by Lucy Ann, who allegedly said, 'Mrs Boldock has sent me to tell you not to tell Sergeant Killington about the poison being missing'.

The next witness was Elizabeth Lacey, who identified herself as the wife of Thomas Lacey, groundsman of Metheringham, and who lived about a quarter of a mile from Mary Buxton. She confirmed that she knew Lucy Ann Buxton and remembered her coming to her house about 9 o'clock in the morning on Friday, 24th April, with the child in her arms. Seeking her advice, an alarmed Lucy Ann Buxton had asked her, 'Whatever is the matter with my child?' Mrs Lacey had told her that the baby was suffering from convulsions, and she should see

Dr Bower, as he was afflicted 'in the same manner as I have heard of other children who have been convulsed'. Her description of those afflictions, like that of Mary Buxton, was explicit and uncomfortable to hear. The child 'appeared to be in pain and uneasy'; 'its mouth was drawn up quite round and it worked its tongue about'; 'when it came out of convulsive fits it screamed'. Also like Mary Buxton, she made it clear that she had not given the child anything to eat or drink whilst they were in her house.

Mrs Lacey said that Lucy Ann 'seemed anxious' and had hoped that the child would get better. She remained at the house for about forty-five minutes, during which time, there was no improvement in the health of John Edward Buxton. At the request of the mother, Mrs Lacey sent her two grandchildren to fetch Mary Buxton from the house of John Greenham's foreman, who came immediately. At about 9.45, they left the house together.

Elizabeth Boldock, widow, also appearing for the second time in front of the coroner, remembered quite vividly the sad events of Friday, 24th April. She recalled Lucy Ann Buxton and her child coming to her house between 11 o'clock and noon to wait for Dr Bower to return. She too was able to describe the dreadful symptoms of violent convulsions and screaming which the child endured up to the final minutes before its untimely death. She also added that Lucy Ann 'seemed much cut up at the child's death'.

There was no reference to the story that Mrs Boldock had advised Lucy Ann Buxton to cover up the missing poison.

John Thomas Buxton, labourer, and brother of Lucy Ann Buxton gave evidence for the first time. On the whole it supported and clarified the deposition of his wife concerning the mysterious saucepan and the search for *Battle's Vermin Killer*.

Mr Buxton had last used the saucepan on Friday 14th April, adding that it was always kept in the stable of his master, Mr Grebby. After using it to wash the horse corn, he had left it on the tub, but at 2 o'clock that afternoon he discovered it had been moved and turned upside-down. Nobody had access to the house except himself, his wife and his sister.

He repeated the story that his father had said something which had initiated a futile search of the house for a packet of *Battle's Vermin Killer*, although like his wife, he did not clarify exactly what his father had said to him.

There was no mention of the significance of the eggs discovered on the table by his wife, but that was explained by the next witness, James Thorpe, who lived with this father in Metheringham. Mr Thorpe remembered finding two eggs in the crew yard at Mr Grebby's farm, and one in the stable. He had taken them to John Buxton, Mr Grebby's groundsman, and placed them on the table. The information about the eggs seemed trivial and contradictory, but that hardly seemed to matter, as his additional comments carried greater significance in terms of the possible administering of poison. James Thorpe had encountered Lucy Ann with her child outside the house, whose door was open, around half-past ten. She had the child in her arms, but 'all was quiet' and she made 'no complaint' about the child being ill.

Dr Bower testified that he had examined the dead body of John Edward Buxton, after being called to the house of Mrs Boldock, at around 1 o'clock, on 24th April. The body of the child was still warm and the 'countenance was perfectly natural', although he noticed that the hands were clenched the thumbs 'drawn downwards towards the palm'.

On 27th April, he had performed a post mortem examination, carefully examining the throat and the bowels, but could discover no inflammation of either; in fact, all the organs of the body were perfectly healthy and he was unable to discover any cause of death.

The stomach and a large portion of the small intestines were placed in a jar, sealed up and packed, and then given to Sergeant Killington.

George Killington, police sergeant for parts of Kesteven and stationed at Metheringham, confirmed that he had received the two jars from Dr Bower, after witnessing him sealing and packing them up. On the same day, he packed them into a box and took them to Lincoln to hand them over to Superintendent Allingham. Also on the same day, he apprehended Lucy Ann Buxton and charged her with the suspected murder of her illegitimate child: to which she made no reply.

The testimony of Sergeant Killington ended with him testifying that on 6th May he went to the shop of J R Battle, in Lincoln, and purchased a threepenny packet of *Battle's Vermin Killer*, before travelling down to London to deliver it to Professor Swaine Taylor at his home in St James Terrace, Regent's Park.

Superintendent John Allingham, also serving parts of Kesteven, testified that he had received the sealed and packed jars from Sergeant Killington on the 27th April, and that he took them to London on 30th April, and gave them to Professor Swaine Taylor at Guy's Hospital.

The final deposition and in many respects the most important one from the point of view of the coroner, was from the eminent toxicologist, Professor Alfred Swaine Taylor. It was a lengthy, detailed and conclusive report, which left little doubt that strychnine poison had been administered to the child.

Professor Swaine Taylor confirmed that he

had received the sealed jars from Superintendent Allingham on 30th April at his laboratory.

The initial observations on the stomach and the coats confirmed the conclusions of Dr Bowes's post mortem that at the time of death it was in a healthy state. On opening up the stomach, he did not discover anything unusual: 'there was no smell of opium, prussic acid, or other volatile poison'. He did, however, note the presence of minute dark particles which had the properties of Prussian blue.

Further tests revealed that the lining membrane of the stomach was healthy, albeit unusually pale: there was no inflammation, ulceration, or other signs of disease.

The intestines were also generally healthy, containing neither blood nor bile, nor any mineral or vegetable substance 'of a suspicious kind'. He did, however, refer once again to the presence of 'the small particles of blue colouring matter' as an area of concern.

The stomach and intestines had been subject to the usual chemical analysis for a variety of poisons which might have caused sudden death, such as prussic acid, morphia, opium, arsenic, antimony and mercury, 'as well as other mineral substances of a noxious kind'.

None of these was found.

However, what he did discover was a small quantity

of strychnine, described by the professor as 'a powerful poison, which is extracted from nux vomica'.

At this point, the London expert referred to the packet of *Battle's Vermin Killer* which Superintendent Allingham had subsequently delivered to him. It was a logical continuation of his report, which at the same time created a sense of the skilled performer moving inexorably towards a dramatic, clinching finale.

The product was a blue coloured powder, contained within yellow paper with printed directions for its use and 'conspicuously marked' with the word 'Poison'. Under the microscope the blue powder, weighing fifteen grains, was found to contain starch granules of wheat flour, mixed with strychnine. The ingestion of only one grain of the powder would be sufficient to cause death to an infant.

His conclusion was that the composition of *Battle's Vermin Killer* – wheat flour coloured with Prussian blue and containing a small quantity of strychnine – were all present in the stomach of the infant, in addition to mucus and the constituents of bread and milk.

The analysis, with its detailed description of both the contents and the packaging of the poison, impressed the coroner's jury sufficiently for it to pass a verdict of Guilty and that Lucy Buxton should be sent for trial at the next Assize session in Lincoln.

The report ended with an apology for mistakenly

informing the reader the previous week that Lucy Ann Buxton had been re-apprehended in Bardney, after her escape from Kesteven Police Station, at the house of Mrs Hird: this should have read Mr Morris.

The report on the resumed inquest which appeared in the *Stamford Mercury* on the same day consisted of shortened versions of the depositions of Mary Buxton, Elizabeth Lacey and Elizabeth Boldock, although it did include the report of Professor Swaine Taylor in full.

The excerpts from the three women were somewhat random and did not make for a very helpful and coherent narrative of their depositions. Perhaps significantly, in terms of creating reader speculation about the case, the report did include the story of the missing mouse powder and the visit of Lucy Ann to report Mrs Boldock's alleged advice to cover up the missing poison, recounted by Mary Buxton.

It also included an additional comment from the expert toxicologist, not recorded by the *Lincolnshire Chronicle*, made in response to a question from the coroner at the end of his report. The professor considered that the symptoms he had observed were consistent with poisoning by strychnine, however, they were also 'consistent with natural disease in children of that age'. As reported, the comment seemed like a passing observation, rather than a concerned caveat.

The resumed inquest was also reported by the *Sleaford Gazette*, but was no more than a duplicate of the version printed in the *Stamford Mercury*.

Trial of Lucy Ann Buxton at Lincoln Assizes, 24th July, 1868, in front of Lord Justice Robert Lush

The earliest and very different reports of the trial appeared in *The Times*, on 27th July, the *Western Daily Press*, published in Bristol, and in the Nottinghamshire-based *Newark Advertiser*, both on 29th July.

The Times report, in the context of the business of the Midland Circuit in Lincoln, was an impressionistic continuous narrative of the case, with little attempt to prioritise or discriminate between the various depositions: the report of Professor Swaine Taylor, for example, was given less space than the evidence relating to the mystery eggs and saucepan. The lack of perspective and sound journalistic judgement was evident in the final paragraph, which described the complete collapse of Lucy Ann Buxton in the dock after hearing her death sentence, but tritely reassured the reader that she 'was dressed in a remarkably smart manner'.

The version published in the Bristol newspaper, and later reproduced by several other newspapers, was a very short, but sympathetic thumbnail sketch of the trial and sentencing of the prisoner, concluding that, 'There was no evidence as to how the poison was administered, but some small circumstances adduced as tending to show that it had been given by the prisoner'.

The early report published in the *Newark Advertiser,* and reprinted a few days later in the *Nottingham Guardian,* was a lengthy, and on the surface, a full account of the trial proceedings. A close examination of the story, however, reveals that the witness statements, for the most part, are a misleading unaltered duplication of the report on the resumed inquest at Metheringham, found in the *Lincolnshire Chronicle* of 15th May. In addition, the careful, systematic report of Professor Swaine Taylor was reduced to an unhelpful eleven line distillation, describing the stomach contents of the dead child and the constituent parts of *Battle's Vermin Killer* only. The only distinctive part of the report, which may or may not have been true, was the unusual expression, allegedly used by the Counsel for the Defence, rooted in St Matthew's Gospel, that there was not 'a single tittle of evidence' to prove the prisoner's guilt. It is perhaps significant that this single quotation was the sole substantiation of the newspaper's claim that Defence Counsel had 'made a most earnest and eloquent appeal to the jury on behalf of the unhappy prisoner'.

Having anticipated the grim drama of a death sentence, perhaps, both the *Lincolnshire Chronicle* and the *Stamford Mercury*, reported the trial in substantial detail, on Friday, 31st July.

The Grand Jury consisted mainly of men already experienced in hearing evidence at capital trials:

Hon A L Melville (Foreman)
Samuel Allenby
Sir Charles Henry John Anderson
John Bromhead
Richard G Ellison
Robert Ellison
J W Fox
Thomas Garfit
Richard Gleed
F L Hopkins
E M Hutton
William Hutton
George Knowles Jarvis
George Augustus Luard
Charles Thomas John Moore
George Nevil(e)
William Parker
Edward Peacock
Wilkinson Peacock
John Reeve
Joseph Shuttleworth

Samuel Wright Wright

The briefing which Lord Justice Lush presented to the Grand Jury was a relaxed one in terms of his assessment of the Calendar, which consisted of the usual number of cases, but not the usual amount of crime: in his estimation, finding a true bill, or not, would only take a short time.

However, he did wish to draw attention to two or three cases, one of which was that of Lucy Ann Buxton, charged with the murder of what he supposed was her illegitimate child. His supposition was correct, as pre-trial newspaper reports had confirmed, but was hardly material evidence in a balanced preamble to the case.

The focus of His Lordship in giving guidance to the Grand Jury, as reported by the *Lincolnshire Chronicle*, was primarily the attention they should give to the report of Professor Swaine Taylor, which was undeniably central to the case: his investigations had discovered the presence of the constituent parts of *Battle's Vermin Killer*, to which the prisoner had access as well as the opportunity to administer, and the symptoms of the deceased child's illness were consistent with strychnine poisoning. On the other hand, however, those same symptoms were also consistent with natural causes, according to the expert toxicologist.

In a weak and somewhat lame defence of Lucy Ann Buxton, his Lordship noted that 'the young woman was attached to her child'.

The *Lincolnshire Chronicle* reported on the trial witness by witness. Most of the evidence was already in the public domain, having been fully reported in the account of the resumed inquest at Metheringham. Whilst what was heard repeated most of the essentials of those depositions, the trial versions occasionally produced some variations which had emerged from cross-examination from both Counsels, as well as some useful new evidence.

The Counsel for the Prosecution was conducted by Mr Lewis Cave, Mr John Mellor and Mr Horace Smith; the Counsel for the Defence by the Honourable Edward Chandos Leigh, Recorder of Stamford since 1864.

Mr Cave opened the trial with a summary of the key points of the case for the Prosecution, although the newspaper provided no details of the speech.

The extensive evidence of Mary Buxton was a repetition of her deposition at Metheringham, with the occasional additional detail, most of it without any great significance. For example, the reason for the journey to buy milk was to feed the baby and it was the grandchildren of Mrs Boldock who alerted her to the medical crisis as she was returning home from buying the milk.

Some of the new details, on the other hand, were potentially significant in either raising questions or furthering suspicions. On her return from her father-in-law's house, for example, after having left Lucy Ann in her house, she had 'found her in the house *all alone*'. When Lucy Ann turned back half way through the walk to buy milk, 'she *did not give any reasons for so doing*'; and further, 'She went in the direction of my house, *but I did not watch her*'.

On the whole, the depositions of Mary Buxton were consistent and coherent, held together with clear recollections of time and place. The only exception to this was her account of who had charge of the baby during the difficulties caused by the absence of Dr Bower. In their factual details, her story changed from one at the initial inquest to another at the resumed inquest and finally to that at the trial, although these minor inconsistences may have been the result of inaccurate or inept reporting.

However, there were three occasions when Mrs Buxton provided interesting new evidence which might have been useful to either a Prosecution narrative of probably Guilty or a Defence narrative of possibly Not Guilty.

She told the court that the *Battle's Vermin Powder* in her possession was wrapped in blue paper with printing on it: this was at variance with the discovery in the fire grate of yellow paper, previously deposed by Mrs Buxton, noted by Professor Swaine Taylor as part of the poisoning narrative and highlighted by the judge in his opening address to the jury. If accurate, it contradicted an important piece of circumstantial evidence; if inaccurate, it undermined the credibility of a key witness. In view of Mary Buxton switching her story back to a yellow package later on in her deposition, it may be, of course, that the wrong colour was merely a confused journalistic recollection of the importance of Prussian blue in considering the evidence.

More significantly, Mary Buxton, it emerged, was in the habit of putting the poison on bread and butter which she carefully laid on shelves and upstairs, presumably as mouse bait. She had deposed several times that her sister-in-law had fed the child with bread, whilst in her house, and further, the constituents of bread had been found in John Edward Buxton's stomach by Professor Swaine Taylor. The window of opportunity had been opened to both Counsels: the feeding of poisoned bread to the infant may have been either a malicious and calculated act of murder or could have been a dreadful, innocent mistake.

The final part of her story of *Battle's Vermin Killer* confirmed to the court that she had last seen the powder on the afternoon of Thursday, 23rd April.

There were various references at the resumed

inquest to eggs appearing in the house. The significance, however, even after hearing an explanation for how they got there, still remained rather elusive. The mystery seemed to be on the same level as that of a saucepan being moved from its usual place, by person unknown.

In Mrs Buxton's new evidence which she 'did not mention at the time' because she 'did not suspect anything was wrong when I got home after the child's death', was her discovery on the fire-back of a piece of egg-shell. She had not used any eggs that day nor did she know of anyone else who had. Her new evidence seemed to explain very little other than the confusion as to whether two or three eggs were found in the house and the discovery of the saucepan in an unexpected place.

Perhaps the most interesting part of Mary Buxton's deposition was not so much what she said, as what she didn't say: there was no mention of the damning evidence that Lucy Ann, on the advice of Mrs Boldock, had told her not to mention the missing poison to Sergeant Killington.

It is not surprising that the Defence Counsel showed no interest in either eggs or saucepans in his cross-examination. Based upon the responses of Mary Buxton, he seemed more interested to discover that Lucy Ann had pressed her to ask the doctor if there was going to be an inquest, to which he had replied that he did not think so; and further, that the child was not seen by any doctor before he had died.

The depositions of both Mrs Lacey and Mrs Boldock produced nothing of note beyond agreeing that Lucy Ann was 'affectionate to the child' and that after he had died on her knee, she was 'very much affected at its death'.

James Thorpe, the purveyor of mystery eggs, appeared before the court, but added nothing new to his deposition, other than a slightly revised time for his encounter with Lucy Ann Buxton and her child outside her brother's house, now recalling it being 'about 10 o'clock or a little after', rather than the more precise ten-thirty.

The deposition of Dr Bower at the inquest had focused upon his observations of the dead child, in particular the clenched hand. In his latest testimony were added details of the post mortem which he carried out on 27th April. His routine examination had revealed nothing to suggest anything other than death by natural causes. He had examined the bowels, but could find no evidence of inflammation and all the major organs were perfectly healthy. He told the court that the causes of convulsions were known to be various, including teething, overloading of the stomach and inflammation of the gums, but he had not found evidence to support any of these explanations.

Under cross-examination from the Defence, Dr Bower remained cautious in his analysis of the ultimate cause of death: 'I cannot say that the convulsions did not arise from natural causes, but I should not expect it'.

According to the report in the *Lincolnshire Chronicle*, nothing new emerged from the depositions of Sergeant Killington and Superintendent Allingham, both of whom had performed their duties, as required by the law.

The report by Professor Taylor, however, did contain material not heard at the resumed inquest, which described in some detail the effects of strychnine on the body, especially that of a small child. When strychnia enters the stomach, he said, it caused death by being absorbed into the bloodstream, but the rate of absorption varied. Sometimes it took only five minutes to act, on other occasions up to thirty minutes. Referring back to a previous case, Professor Swaine Taylor noted that a sixteenth part of one grain of the poison had been known to kill a child aged between four and five years in the space of four hours. In addition, it was important to grasp that the strychnine found in the stomach of a victim would not be the cause of death, but the amount absorbed into the bloodstream, which was undetectable.

He also described the distressing effects of the powerful poison on the human body. Convulsions start with a sudden jerk of the head, the arms and the legs, as the body becomes quite stiff 'in a bow-like form'. The fits continue more and more frequently until the person who has swallowed the poison dies from nervous exhaustion: the more frequent the fits and the longer they last, the sooner the victim dies.

Interestingly, in this version of the Professor's deposition he refers to the possibility that the convulsions were produced by natural causes, but in less cautious terms than previously recorded. In the case of such convulsions, he would have expected to have found evidence for such a conclusion after death – and clearly he had found no such evidence. If correctly reported, the conclusion embedded in the report was unambiguously explicit: 'Strychnia must have been swallowed in the form of the vermin killer'.

The closing statement by Mr Mellor for the Prosecution, as reported, was a restrained and laconic mixture of melancholic sympathy, real or contrived, and grim factuality culled from Professor Taylor's report.

He did not wish to make the case 'bleaker than it really was', but he wished to remind the jury how easy it was to administer poison and how hard it was to detect. He also wished to highlight what they had heard from the expert scientific account, especially in relation to the detection of a poison absorbed into the bloodstream as the true cause of death, not the quantity discovered in the stomach after death. Perhaps taking the lead from the opening remarks of the judge, the Prosecution strategy appeared to be one of suggesting that the key evidence to consider was not so much the circumstantial nature of the anecdotal, as the factual reliability of the scientific.

The summary report of the 'long and earnest appeal on behalf of the prisoner' by the Defence was disappointingly short to the point of being non-existent, especially for any reader interested in the arguments which might have been used by Chandos Leigh, ingenious or otherwise, to save Lucy Ann Buxton from the hangman.

Greater column space was given to the response of Mr Justice Lush after hearing the verdict of Guilty from the Foreman of the Jury. He entirely concurred with the decision and advised the prisoner, employing the usual empty judicial formula, that she must prepare for a great change and seek the pardon of the Almighty, which she might not hope for in court.

According to the newspaper, on hearing the sentence of death, Lucy Ann Buxton fainted, and on recovering, 'screamed and moaned bitterly', and had to be carried out of court. It was a description reminiscent of Hetty Sorrell's reaction to being condemned to death for the crime of infanticide in George Eliot's *Adam Bede*.

The account of the trial in the *Lincolnshire*

Chronicle was reported in both its Friday and Saturday editions of 31st July and 1st August respectively.

In the later edition, it also published a letter, for the most part full of sincere, pious platitudes, requesting all Christians to unite in prayer for the young woman, Lucy Buxton, 'now lying under sentence of death for the murder of her child'. Specifically, it suggested that all clergymen and other Christian ministers 'would do well to commend her to the intercession of their people, both in their public and private devotions', proposing that supplications should be offered up at either 7.30 am or 9.30 am, or as near to those times as possible.

The letter was also a special plea for 'the excellent chaplain of the gaol, who would be strengthened and encouraged in his awfully responsible work by the assurance of special Divine help being asked for him and for her whom he is seeking to prepare for eternity'.

The letter was signed by OPS, almost certainly a member of the clerical circle of Lincoln Cathedral, who attached a prayer for the reader to use.

The prayer was an earnest desire for the redemption of the condemned woman, through the removal of 'all ignorance and hardness of heart' and the granting of 'an unfeigned repentance for all her past sins'. It was also a request for a blessing to be given to the gaol Chaplain that his words might not be spoken in vain, but be a source of everlasting salvation for Lucy Ann Buxton.

The letter was perhaps a greater source of comfort to the gaol Chaplain, Henry Richter, than it was to the wretched prisoner, now condemned to be the first woman to be executed in private, under the terms of the *Capital Punishment Amendment Act* of 1868.

The trial was reported differently in the *Stamford Mercury*, written as a continuous narrative of what was heard, with few references to the source of the information presented to the court, other than a shorter version of Professor Swaine Taylor's evidence.

It did, however, provide the reader with a digest of the Prosecution case against the prisoner, as well as particulars from the summing up of both Counsels at the end of the trial.

According to the *Stamford Mercury*, the main line of argument by the Counsel for the Prosecution, was that Lucy Ann Buxton, after unexpectedly leaving her sister, went back to the house and administered the poison to her child 'immediately before taking it to Mrs Lacey's'. This was proved by 'the lad who was collecting eggs from the farm yard' who had seen the prisoner standing by the door between the time she left her sister-in-law on the road and the time she went to Mrs Lacey's house; further, one of the three eggs which he had put on the table in the house was missing. In addition, a piece of paper in which the vermin powder had been wrapped, and which had been seen a day or two before in the dairy, was found in the fire grate, along with a piece of egg shell. It was also proved that a small saucepan had been removed from the stable and used by the prisoner during the absence of Mary Buxton.

The version of the final address to the jury by Mr Mellor as reported by the *Stamford Mercury*, was similar to that reported in the *Lincolnshire Chronicle*, in that it created an impression of sympathy for the young woman's plight: if the jury found her Not Guilty, he proclaimed, 'there was no person in that court who would rejoice more sincerely than himself'. However, whilst it was not for Mr Mellor to find a motive for the crime, he did suggest that it might be that 'the child was illegitimate and was upon her hands'. In this version of Mr Mellor's remarks, there was no specific reference to the importance of following the science when reaching a verdict.

The report of the closing arguments of the Counsel for the Defence was more detailed. The Honourable Chandos Leigh's speech, as reported, seemed to take refuge in the plodding safety of text book legal formulae, rather than adopting the rhetorical skill and passion necessary to produce a verdict in favour of the prisoner. He began by reminding the jury that the life of Lucy Ann Buxton depended very much upon himself and them. Their first task was to decide whether the child had died from the administration of poison, or not. In addition, before finding the prisoner guilty they must be satisfied 'beyond all reasonable doubt – not upon suspicion – or mere presumption – that she administered it wilfully, intentionally, and with malice aforethought'. If correctly reported, the opening gambits of the speech gave the unfortunate impression of an elementary lesson on the subject of sufficient evidence, presented to an experienced jury which was probably very well aware of such key terms of reference in reaching a verdict.

The second part of the closing speech attempted to present points in favour of the prisoner, but seemingly with little conviction. In the first place, there was no evidence to prove that she had administered the poison. Secondly, there was no motive for the crime, especially in the light of the child 'having been well-received by all the prisoner's friends and was beloved by her'. The lack of evidence beyond the circumstantial and the absence of a clear motive were the generic commonplaces of Defence Counsel pleading, which to be effective required the support of a probing examination of the evidence, if doubts were to be put in the minds of a jury. Ironically, he had first-hand knowledge of such robust probing, when Mr James Fitzjames Stephen, a colleague on the Midland Circuit, had swayed a jury in favour of acquitting Elizabeth Dodds in 1860, by exploiting the lack of a clear motive and irrefutable evidence with acute analysis and skilful rhetoric.

The comment made by the judge in his summing up of the trial that Lucy Ann Buxton had enjoyed 'a most able defence' and that everything that could be done for her had been done, seemed a somewhat generous assessment of the performance of the Honourable Edward Chandos Leigh.

The *Stamford Mercury* also reported that Mr Justice Lush, during the course of 'a lengthy and careful summing up', told the jury that if they thought the child died from poisoning and that the prisoner administered it, he could not see how it might have got into its stomach by accident. If true, the assertion seemed to ignore the testimony of Mary Buxton that it was her common practice to lace bread with vermin killer, which was left in various accessible spaces in the house, including the dairy, and that the child was fed with bread and water by its mother whilst at her house. It also seemed to dismiss the speculative contention of the Counsel for the Defence reported in the trial summary of *The Times* and the *Hull and Eastern Counties Herald*, that poison might have accidentally found its way into the baby's food.

The jury did not feel the need to leave the box, only consulting for a short time before reaching a Guilty verdict, with which the judge concurred 'entirely'. Mr

Justice Lush, addressing the prisoner before passing a death sentence, assured her that she had been served by 'a most patient and intelligent jury who have given an anxious consideration of the evidence'. In view of their rapid deliberation without leaving the box and an astonishing development which took place a few days later, it seemed a rather uncritical assessment of the day's proceedings.

The final paragraph of the report noted that during the trial Lucy Ann Buxton 'behaved with self-possession', but on being sentenced she was overcome and collapsed into her seat in the dock. As also reported in the *Lincolnshire Chronicle*, the trial ended melodramatically, when the condemned woman was 'carried away shrieking to her cell'.

It was with unintended irony that the *Stamford Mercury* also reported that the prisoner had broken down in tears during the speech by the Honourable Mr Chandos Leigh, whose rhetorical skills in defending an admittedly difficult case were either underreported or woefully inadequate.

The decision to employ the distinguished Recorder of Stamford to defend Lucy Ann Buxton, made by her solicitors, Messrs Toynbee and Larken of Lincoln, was in some respects a natural one. He was a man of many years' experience on the Midland Circuit and had been involved in two high profile poisoning cases in Lincolnshire in the early 1860s:

the trial of John and Elizabeth Garner from Mareham le Fen, alongside Mr James Fitzjames Stephen, and that of Elizabeth Vamplew, from Grimoldby.

On the other hand, it was arguably a choice fraught with potential attendant difficulties.

In his book, *Over Fen and Wold*, published in 1898, the bemused travel writer, James John Hissey, described Metheringham as 'an out-of-the-world, forsaken-looking, little town': the description found in both White and Kelly decades earlier of 'a large improving village' seemed to have been either optimistic or premature, as far as Hissey and his travelling companion were concerned, as they were initially unable to locate the place in their copy of *Paterson's Roads*, leading to the exasperated and scathing comment, 'why, or how, it existed at all was a puzzle to us'.

The world of Metheringham in 1868, or more precisely, the world of the Tan Vats area of Metheringham Fen, could not have been further away from the cosseted and entitled world of the aristocratic Honourable Edward Chandos Leigh, of Stoneleigh Abbey, Warwickshire. Educated at Harrow and Oriel College, Oxford, he was more of a gentleman with a keen interest in cricket, than a champion of criminal justice, more a man who accidentally ended up being a barrister of the Inner Temple, because he did not want to be a clergyman.

By his own account, in his 1913 autobiography, *Bar, Bat and Bit*, his decision to enter the Inner Temple was based upon 'the impulse of the moment' and his legal career upon the hope that 'it might be useful to me if I entered political life or if I wanted to get some place out of a Whig Government'.

Whilst fashioning a successful legal career for himself, he achieved greater contemporary and posthumous recognition having played cricket for Harrow, Oxford and the MCC, prompting the reviewer of his autobiography in *The Spectator* to comment, quite rightly, that 'his heart was chiefly in sport'.

Media reports of his performance in the courtroom often created a sense of him ponderously and pedantically delivering a tedious lecture, unaware of the need to engage with his audience on anything other than on a pedestrian, formal level. His opening remarks as Recorder of Stamford addressed to a Grand Jury, reported in the *Stamford Mercury*, 22nd October, 1869, for example, seemed to typify his judicial style. His prefatory remarks on the two cases up for review, consisting of a dry, point by point account of the main clauses of the *Habitual Criminal Act* of 1869, including those sections related to the theft of scrap metal, seemed both disproportionate and irrelevant to the theft of a shawl on the one hand and a pair of boots on the other.

Reprieve of Lucy Ann Buxton from the Death Sentence, received by the Governor at Lincoln Castle Prison, 4th August, 1868

The extant *Prison Journals* of the Governor, the Surgeon, the Chaplain and the Matron of Lincoln Castle prison often provide valuable insights into the daily behaviours and attitudes of the prisoners convicted of a capital crime. The pained concern of Eliza Joyce for the family which she was leaving behind in 1844, the volatile mental health of Mary Ann Milner in 1847 and the continuous determined refusal of Priscilla Biggadike to admit any wrongdoing in 1868, for example, would all have been lost without these professional documents.

The entries in the various journals which relate to Lucy Ann Buxton are an interesting and useful record of her time as a prisoner, but unfortunately provide little sense of her as a human being, even during the time between her sentence to death and her reprieve, just days before the scheduled execution. If the entries in the prison journals are an accurate reflection of her time in Lincoln Castle, she said very little to anyone.

It may be, of course, that the silences of Lucy Ann, suggesting either resignation or indifference, capture the essence of her at the time – a young woman whose identity had been stripped out by the hazards of life and who had been finally reduced to a stupefied spectator trapped in the judicial process. The apparently throwaway comment by the *Stamford Mercury*, in a short article on the delayed removal of Lucy Ann Buxton from Lincoln, published on 28th August, that she was 'not one of the demonstrative sort', may well have contained a good deal of truth.

The first mention of Lucy Ann Buxton in the Governor's *Journal* was not until 24th July, the day of her sentencing at the Assizes, recording that on her return to prison she had been placed in cell C2 and that her warder was to be Hannah Dowse.

According to the Governor, during her first two nights in the condemned cell, the prisoner appeared to sleep well, but on hearing on 27th July that the time of her execution had been fixed for Friday, 7th August, at noon, she 'was very much distressed and said that she had little thought she should come to this'.

For the most part, other than occasional reports about her health and change of diet from the Surgeon, Edward Farr Broadbent, the remainder of the entries by James Foster in his *Journal* are mainly copies of administrative documents relating to Lucy Ann. On 27th July, he wrote to the Home Secretary advising him on the proposed date of the execution; and the following day, he sent the Home Office copies of the two Assize Calendars containing the sentences of the prisoners, along with newspaper cuttings 'containing Assize Intelligence'.

On 4th of August, he acknowledged receipt of a letter from Whitehall, dated 3rd August, which had informed him of the 'respite' given to Lucy Ann Buxton, and he mentions breaking the news to her at 10 o'clock that morning, before ordering her removal to an ordinary cell. There was no record of any reaction to her life being spared, although by a happy coincidence later that day, she was visited by her two sisters, Maria Gauby and Mary Ann Riley, in the company of two aunts, Mary Key and Maria Morris, as well as by Mary Abbot, the housekeeper of Thomas Buxton. Presumably, the five visitors had arrived thinking that it would be to say their final farewells to a condemned prisoner, her father having visited her on 31st July for the same purpose.

On 27th August, Lucy Ann Buxton was informed by the Governor, that the final order in her case had been received and that she had been sentenced to penal servitude for life. Again, there was no recorded response by the prisoner to her impending fate.

The final business, as far as James Foster was concerned, was a letter to the Honourable Adolphus Frederick Liddell, Under-Secretary of State for the Home Office, requesting an order for the removal of five prisoners to a 'convict depot': Henry Doubleday (ten years), John Simpson (seven years), Thomas Dowse (ten years), Carl Blumberry (ten years) and Lucy Buxton (life).

The five prisoners were eventually removed to Millbank prison on 23rd September, the process having probably been held up by the eruption of a skin disease on the back and chest of Lucy Ann Buxton, and her subsequent bed rest and treatment with an itch ointment by the Surgeon.

Other than the unfortunate skin problem, the journals of the Matron, Sarah Foster, wife of the Governor, and the Surgeon, Edward Farr Broadbent, record very little about Lucy Ann Buxton, beyond such day to day mundanities as a change of diet and her being treated for constipation with 'a dose of house medicine'.

The *Journal* of the Reverend Henry Richter records numerous meetings with Lucy Ann, as part of his daily work of spiritual support for the prisoners: after her being condemned to hang, he frequently visited her both in the morning and in the evening to advise her. In addition, some of his sermons delivered in the prison chapel, referred to her conviction and impending death, but were probably meant as a powerful cautionary warning to the other prisoners, rather than offered as any kind of uplifting spiritual consolation for Lucy Ann.

His many visits did not seem to have elicited any meaningful verbal responses from the condemned woman and so her words to the Governor concerning her unexpected misfortunes, remain the only explicit record of her thoughts and feelings. Several comments which the Chaplain made about her seem to confirm that little, if anything, was said, or that alternatively, she really did not have anything much to say to him.

The day after being condemned to death, Henry Richter visited her and noted that she 'does not seem much affected by her condition'. Visiting her again, the following day, after having delivered a 'sermon and discourse in reference to the condition of Lucy Buxton' to the assembled prisoners in the chapel, he thought that she was now 'more sensible of her condition', although without elaborating upon his satisfied assertion.

Two days later, on 28th July, the Chaplain was congratulating himself upon having made some progress with the Lucy Ann: 'Made, I think, some impression upon her; some evidence of feeling about her'. The terms are vague and slightly curious in their emphasis upon the display of feelings, but once again, there is no elaboration of his comment.

In the *Journal* entry for 31st July, the Reverend Richter records his disappointment that the condemned prisoner showed 'no great appearance of feeling about her', during his evening visit. What follows perhaps suggests an over-optimistic interpretation of the difficulties, from a man seeking an explanation of, or remedy for, such tearless, sullen silence: 'I trust that she is both resigned to her fate and is earnestly preparing herself for it'.

The following day, he explained the sacrament to her, 'with the hope that she will be prepared to receive it'. He also noted, with a very cautious optimism, that she 'showed some emotion'. What exactly that emotion was he did not explain, but it clearly represented progress of sorts to the Chaplain.

After her reprieve, the Reverend gentleman continued to advise her up the point of her discharge to Millbank prison, mainly on the theme of the mercy which had been extended to her and the hope that she 'would be constantly mindful of it'.

No doubt, his spiritual conference with Lucy Ann Buxton on 7th August would have been especially focused on the gratitude she should now feel, as that was the day she should have been executed, as he noted in his *Journal* for that day.

On 6th September, along with a debtor by the name of Richard Chapman, Lucy Ann Buxton did eventually receive the sacrament. It was a triumph of sorts for a Chaplain struggling to make sense of a woman convicted of the inexplicable crime of poisoning her infant son, and one which was probably much needed in the scandalous aftermath of the suicide of Mary Ann Milner just hours before her execution, in 1847. At the same time, it was one which was of little use in preparing him for his spectacular confrontational failures when trying to deal with Priscilla Biggadike, which began just four weeks later.

The fullest report of the reprieve of Lucy Ann Buxton was published in the *Lincolnshire Chronicle*, 7th August, three days after the Governor of Lincoln prison had received a letter of confirmation from the Home Secretary, the Right Honourable George Gathorne Hardy, MP for Oxford University.

As well as informing its readers of the prime movers in the process of the commutation, the report manages to steer a steady course between recognising both the mitigating quality of mercy shown towards the condemned woman and the need to protect the most vulnerable in society.

The petition to the Home Secretary was prepared by Messrs Toynbee and Larken, the Lincoln solicitors of Lucy Ann Buxton, and was forwarded on Monday, 3rd August. It was signed by numerous people, but mainly by citizens of Lincoln who were opposed to the death penalty, as might have been expected. What would not have been expected was that it was also signed by all members of the Grand Jury who, as the newspaper pointed out, had condemned her to death without any recommendation of mercy.

As well as the petition prepared by the Lincoln solicitors, the newspaper mentioned that there were also three other petitions to save the life of Lucy Ann

Buxton. One was extensively signed at Metheringham 'where the unfortunate woman was well-known'; another by the magistrates of the city of Lincoln; and a fourth one had been prepared for signing by the Lincoln Corporation. The latter two petitions were never sent as Messrs Toynbee and Larken received a telegram from the Home Office on the Monday evening of 3rd August stating that the prisoner had been reprieved, followed by a communication on the Tuesday morning, informing the solicitors that 'the case had been taken into serious consideration, and that the Home Secretary felt justified in recommending her Majesty to commute the sentence to penal servitude for life'.

The newspaper did not provide any further details of the other three petitions in the report, but did carry an article on a different page relating to the quarterly meeting of the Lincoln Corporation at the Guildhall on Tuesday, 4th August. Amongst the business for the day was a request from the Mayor to the Town Clerk to prepare a petition 'respecting a commutation of the capital sentence on Lucy Buxton', but as a reprieve had come down that morning, the Town Clerk suggested that it was no longer necessary. The Council agreed and the decision to abandon the petition was agreed.

The information that the Grand Jury had signed a petition to countermand their own jurisdiction was a surprising development in the story of Lucy Ann Buxton. A further ironic twist was added by the mover of the petition in the meeting of the Corporation being John Richard Battle, the Mayor, and also the proprietor of *Battle's Vermin Killer*.

According to the report, Lucy Ann, who was 'quite prepared to atone for her shocking crime on the scaffold', received the news of her reprieve 'with great composure': the reporter seemed to know a good deal more about the prisoner than the Reverend Henry Richter.

Moving towards its final reflections upon the unfolding events, the report suggested that the act of clemency by the Crown was clear evidence that support for capital punishment was waning. However, it also insisted that the threat of the death penalty was necessary in cases where victims had been unable to protect themselves.

The final sentence claimed both the moral high ground and, at the same time, reassured its readers that a reprieve was not a let-off. The newspaper did not intend to dwell upon the background of Lucy Ann Buxton, as it believed that 'a life of misery will be ample punishment for her unnatural crime'.

The tact and delicacy concerning the subject of the 'antecedents' of the reprieved prisoner were clearly not an issue for Thomas Beggs, the Secretary of the Society for the Abolition of Capital Punishment, whose open letter on the case was published in various newspapers between 5th and 8th August, strongly suggested that 'antecedents' were very much at the heart of the matter.

The occasion of the robust letter was Beggs and his committee having received several short communications urging their intervention on behalf of 'the wretched girl, Lucy Buxton, who is lying under sentence of death at Lincoln'. Beggs was aware that a memorial was being prepared in Lincoln and had himself already addressed the Home Secretary, 'asking him to recommend the case to the merciful consideration of her Majesty'. Whilst assuring the reader that he did not wish to interfere with the due process of the law, he urged those with any influence to exert it on the prisoner's behalf.

Despite the urgency of the matter, Thomas Beggs seemed optimistic, persuaded that after all the circumstances had been considered, her life would probably be spared, as there had been no executions for infanticide for some years, including cases 'more aggravated than this'. The circumstances, according to Thomas Beggs, included the sorry story of her antecedents, in both senses of the word, and which on first hearing, 'may close the ears of mercy'.

What followed was a biographical sketch of the misfortunes of Lucy Ann Buxton, most of it undeniably true, some of it only possibly true and other parts which were a probable convenient journalistic fabrication. According to Beggs, Lucy Ann had given birth to three illegitimate children, one of them in Lincoln gaol, when she was serving a sentence for robbery: all three children had 'disappeared in a suspicious manner'. In addition to the robbery, she had been previously imprisoned in Leeds for theft. The final 'dark side of the picture' was that she had once escaped from a lock-up and 'at another time', she had attempted suicide.

On the other hand, he suggested, accusation should be tempered by commiseration, in that she was a twenty-two year old woman whose mother had been convicted of a robbery thirteen years ago, when Lucy Ann was only nine years of age. The chronology was wrong, but Beggs made the point that the impact of such a 'dark domestic history' on a girl 'at the most tender period of her life' was decisive enough to cast doubt on her accountability for what she had done.

There is no doubting the sincerity and earnestness of Thomas Beggs, but it is clear that the more lurid and dubious elements of his biographical sketch of Lucy Ann Buxton, were taken from the report in the *Stamford Mercury* of 31st July. The report informed its readers that a memorial to save the life of Lucy Ann Buxton was currently in preparation and in addition provided them with an extensive account of her life, prior to the alleged murder. Amongst the established facts related to her various court appearances, the newspaper included the improbable claims relating to the mysterious disappearance of her illegitimate children and a failed suicide attempt.

It was only surprising that the narrative of Thomas Beggs, in the section on Ann Buxton, did not include the fact that she was hopelessly addicted to opium: it might have made a further telling contribution to his narrative of 'dark domestic history'. Perhaps significantly, the detail did not appear in the report published in the *Stamford Mercury* utilised by Thomas Beggs.

It was a busy year for Thomas Beggs in his dealings with Lincoln in that he was required to argue the abolitionist cause again in the popular press, in December, 1868, to plead clemency for Priscilla Biggadike, who was similarly only days away from being hanged for murder.

The rapidity with which the decision was made by the Home Secretary to reprieve Lucy Ann Buxton, and then acted upon, was probably determined by the weight of support from such public figures as Thomas Beggs, as well as by the urgent fact that the day of execution was imminent.

More speculatively, it may be that political, social and personal connections also played a part in the efficiency of the process. The *Lincolnshire Chronicle* mentioned, in passing, that Lucy Ann was unaware that strenuous efforts were being made on her behalf to have her sentence commuted. Specifically, that her Defence Counsel, the Honourable Edward Chandos Leigh, was working alongside her solicitors to persuade the Home Secretary to reprieve her. Perhaps it was just a coincidence, but both the Honourable Edward Chandos Leigh and the Right Honourable George Gathorne Hardy, were graduates of Oriel College, Oxford and both were barristers of the Inner Temple.

The story of the reprieve of Lucy Ann Buxton was covered less fully by the *Stamford Mercury*, 7th August, beginning somewhat dramatically with the observation that the officials of Lincoln Castle 'had been spared the horror of strangling a young woman'. The focus of the report was not so much the mechanics of the reprieve process and its key players, as the attitude of the prisoner to her impending death. She had 'remained perfectly passive' and 'did not appear at all alarmed': without any helpful further commentary, the information was ambiguous, but to some extent complements the elusive spare, blank image of the young woman created by the Chaplain's *Journal*.

The *Sleaford Gazette*, published the following day, merely duplicated the report in the *Stamford Mercury*, whilst the eighteen word notice of the reprieve in the *Grantham Journal*, bordered on the politely indifferent.

It is frustrating that the Home Office documents relating to the reprieve of Lucy Ann Buxton seem to have been lost. The diary of the Home Secretary, George Gathorne Hardy, is equally unhelpful in its absence of any reference to the reprieve of Lucy Ann Buxton. If the diary entries of the Home Secretary for the end of July are reliable, Hardy was more concerned with parliamentary business, the uncomfortably hot weather and dining at the Carlton Club than with the judicial fate of an obscure woman somewhere in Lincolnshire. Reference is made in passing to the business of the Home Office, which was providing 'plenty to do', but does not record anything specific. On 1st August, Hardy was in Whitehall 'for a short time', but then went to see 'the extinction of the Parliament', after which he left London until 25th August. It may be that the dissolution of Parliament that day distracted Hardy from the day to day running of the Home Office and that the business of managing the paperwork of the Buxton reprieve had, in any case, been left in the capable hands of Adolphus Liddell, the Under-Secretary of State, and his underling civil servants.

The final definition of the identity of Lucy Ann Buxton is to be found in the entries in the *Millbank Register of Female Prisoners*, which record, not entirely accurately, her journey through the prison system:

Register Number: *5438*
Name: *Lucy Buxton*
Age: *22*
Married or Single: *Single*
Read or Write: *Imperfectly*
Trade: *Servant*
Convicted When: *22nd July, 1868*
Convicted Where: *Lincoln*
Crime: *Wilful Murder*
Sentence: *Life*
Received When: *23rd September, 1868*
Received from What Gaol: *Lincoln Castle*
Substance of Gaoler's Report: *Once convicted; once summarily*
Removed When: *13th March, 1869*
Removed Whither: *Brixton Prison*

Register Number: *5934*
Name: *Lucy Buxton*
Age: *22*
Married or Single: *Single*
Read or Write: *Imperfectly*
Trade: *Servant*
Convicted When: *22nd July, 1868*
Convicted Where: *Lincoln*
Crime: *Murder of Male Child*
Sentence: *Life*
Received When: *17th December, 1869*

Received from What Gaol: *Brixton*
Substance of Gaoler's Report: *Two previous convictions*
Removed When: *10th June, 1870*
Removed Whither: *Woking Prison*

In the column recording the length of the sentence given to Prison Register Number 5934, a later hand has written 'Death recorded'.

The curt epitaph, only two words short of silence, seems sadly apposite.

Appendix

Key players in the Lucy Ann Buxton story

ABBOT, Mary. Housekeeper to Thomas Buxton. Visited Lucy Ann Buxton in Lincoln prison.

ALLENBY, Samuel. Served on Grand Jury at the trial of Lucy Ann Buxton, at the Lincoln Assizes. Resident of Cadwell Hall.

ALLINGHAM, Superintendent John. Gave evidence at resumed inquest into the death of John Edward Buxton. Delivered sealed jars to Professor Swaine Taylor in London. Resident of Kesteven Police Station.

ANDERSON, Sir Charles Henry John. Served on Grand Jury at the trial of Lucy Ann Buxton, at the Lincoln Assizes. Resident of Lea Hall, near Gainsborough.

ASHTON, Thomas. Police Superintendent. Searched the house of Ann Buxton on suspicion of theft from the shop of John Norton, draper, in Lincoln.

BAILEY, John. Warder of Leeds City Gaol, produced a certificate from the Clerk of the Peace for Leeds at second hearing of the case against Lucy Ann Buxton for robbery from the house of George Hardy, which confirmed that she had served a sentence in Leeds for stealing a watch.

BATTLE, John Richard. Mayor of Lincoln. Presiding magistrate with William Rudgard at initial hearing of Lucy Ann Buxton for robbery from the house of George Hardy, and also at the second hearing, a week later, with J. Harvey. Owner of chemist shop located on the High Street, Lincoln, and manufacturer of *Battle's Vermin Killer*.

BOLDOCK, Elizabeth. Widow. Gave evidence at the initial and resumed inquests into the death of John Edward Buxton, and at the trial of Lucy Ann Buxton, at the Lincoln Assizes. Resident of Metheringham Fen.

BOSWORTH, Elizabeth Ann. Servant of George Hardy. Witness to robbery from the house of George Hardy by Lucy Ann Buxton. Resident of Lincoln.

BOWER, Dr William. Surgeon. Resident of Drury Street, Metheringham.

BROADBENT, Edward Farr. Surgeon. Attended Lucy Ann Buxton in Lincoln Castle prison.

BROMHEAD, John. Magistrate. Remanded Lucy Ann Buxton to Kesteven Police Station on suspicion of child murder. Served on Grand Jury at the trial of Lucy Ann Buxton, at the Lincoln Assizes. Resident of The Close, Lincoln.

BUXTON, Ann. Mother of Lucy Ann Buxton, convicted of shoplifting and imprisoned in Lincoln prison. Resident of Tan Vats, Metheringham Fen.

BUXTON, John Edward. Illegitimate son of Lucy Ann Buxton.

BUXTON, John Thomas. Labourer. Brother of Lucy Ann Buxton. Gave evidence at resumed inquest into the death of John Edward Buxton.

BUXTON, Mary, sister-in-law of Lucy Ann Buxton, gave evidence at the initial and resumed inquests into the death of John Edward Buxton, and at the trial of Lucy Ann Buxton, at the Lincoln Assizes.

BUXTON, Thomas. Father of Lucy Ann Buxton, publican. Resident of Tan Vats, Metheringham Fen.

BUXTON, Thomas Frederick. Illegitimate son of Lucy Ann Buxton. Resident of Tan Vats, Metheringham Fen.

BUXTON, John Edward. Illegitimate son of Lucy

Ann Buxton. Died from strychnine poisoning. Resident of Tan Vats, Metheringham Fen.

CAVE, Lewis. Counsel for the Prosecution at the trial of Lucy Ann Buxton, at the Lincoln Assizes.

CLARKE, N R. Recorder. Sentenced Ann Buxton at Lincoln Quarter Sessions to eight months in prison for theft from the shop of John Norton.

DOWSE, Hannah. Warder assigned to Lucy Ann Buxton at Lincoln prison.

DRAYCOTT, Henry. Shop assistant to John Norton, draper.

ELLISON, Richard G. Banker. Served on Grand Jury at the trial of Lucy Ann Buxton, at the Lincoln Assizes. Resident of Sudbrooke Holme .

ELLISON, Robert. Served on Grand Jury at the trial of Lucy Ann Buxton, at the Lincoln Assizes.

FOSTER, James: Governor of Lincoln Castle prison.

FOX, J W. Served on Grand Jury at the trial of Lucy Ann Buxton, at the Lincoln Assizes.

GARFIT, Thomas. Banker. Served on Grand Jury at the trial of Lucy Ann Buxton, at the Lincoln Assizes. Resident of Skirbeck, Boston.

GAUBY, Maria. Sister of Lucy Ann Buxton. Visited her at Lincoln prison.

GLEED, Captain Richard. Served on Grand Jury at the trial of Lucy Ann Buxton, at the Lincoln Assizes. Resident of Park House, Donington.

HARDY, George. Butcher. Former employer of

Lucy Ann Buxton. Resident of Magpies Square, Lincoln.

HARDY, Right Honourable George Gathorne. Home Secretary. Reprieved Lucy Ann Buxton.

HARDY, Thomas. Son of George Hardy. Witness to robbery by Lucy Ann Buxton from the family home. Resident of Magpies Square, Lincoln.

HARVEY, J. Presiding magistrate with J R Battle at second hearing of Lucy Ann Buxton for robbery from the house of George Hardy.

HAYLAND, Dr Thomas. Retired surgeon. Resident of 1 High Street, Metheringham.

HITCHINS, James. Coroner at inquest into the death of Ann Buxton, held at Metheringham.

HOPKINS, Frederick Lyons. Served on Grand Jury at the trial of Lucy Ann Buxton, at the Lincoln Assizes. Resident of Wide Bargate, Boston.

HUTTON, E M. Served on Grand Jury at the trial of Lucy Ann Buxton, at the Lincoln Assizes.

HUTTON, William. Served on Grand Jury at the trial of Lucy Ann Buxton, at the Lincoln Assizes. Resident of Gate Burton Hall.

JARVIS, George Knowles. Served on Grand Jury at the trial of Lucy Ann Buxton, at the Lincoln Assizes. Resident of Doddington Hall.

KEY, Mary. Aunt of Lucy Ann Buxton. Visited her in Lincoln prison.

KILLINGTON, George. Police Sergeant stationed

at Metheringham. Gave evidence at the resumed inquest into the death of John Edward Buxton. Purchased and delivered to Professor Swaine Taylor in London a packet of *Battle's Vermin Killer*.

LACEY, Elizabeth. Wife of Thomas Lacey, groundsman, gave evidence at the inquest into the death of John Edward Buxton and at the trial of Lucy Ann Buxton, at the Lincoln Assizes. Resident of Metheringham Fen.

LEIGH, Honourable Edward Chandos. Counsel for the Defence at the trial of Lucy Ann Buxton, at the Lincoln Assizes. Resident of Stoneleigh Abbey, Warwickshire.

LILBURN, William. Police Detective. Arrested Lucy Ann Buxton in Lincoln for suspected robbery from the house of George Hardy.

LUARD, George Augustus. Served on Grand Jury at the trial of Lucy Ann Buxton, at the Lincoln Assizes. Resident of Blyborough Hall.

LUSH, Lord Justice Robert. Presiding judge at the trial of Lucy Ann Buxton, at the Lincoln Assizes.

MELLOR, J W. Counsel for the Prosecution at the trial of Lucy Ann Buxton, at the Lincoln Assizes.

MELVILLE, Honourable Alexander Leslie. Banker. Served as Foreman on the Grand Jury at the trial of Lucy Ann Buxton, at the Lincoln Assizes. Resident of Branston Hall.

MITCHINSON, George. Coroner presiding at the inquest into the death of John Edward Buxton, at the White Horse Public House, Metheringham.

MELLOR, John William. Counsel for the Prosecution at the trial of Lucy Ann Buxton at the Lincoln Assizes.

MOORE, Colonel Charles Thomas John. Served on Grand Jury at the trial of Lucy Ann Buxton, at the Lincoln Assizes. Resident of Frampton Hall.

MORRIS, Maria. Aunt of Lucy Ann Buxton. Visited her in Lincoln prison.

NEVILLE, George. Served on Grand Jury at the trial of Lucy Ann Buxton, at the Lincoln Assizes. Resident of Stubton Hall.

NORTON, John. Draper, located at St Peter at Arches, Lincoln.

PARKER, William. Served on Grand Jury at the trial of Lucy Ann Buxton, at the Lincoln Assizes. Resident of Hanthorpe House, Bourne.

RILEY, Mary Ann. Sister of Lucy Ann Buxton. Visited her in Lincoln prison.

TAYLOR, Professor Alfred Swaine. Fellow of the College of Physicians and Professor of Medical Jurisprudence at Guy's Hospital, London. Gave expert evidence at resumed inquest into the death of John Edward Buxton.

PEACOCK, Edward. Served on Grand Jury at the trial of Lucy Ann Buxton, at the Lincoln Assizes. Resident of Manor House, Bottesford.

PEACOCK, Reverend Wilkinson Affleck. Served on Grand Jury at the trial of Lucy Ann Buxton, at the Lincoln Assizes. Resident of Rectory House, Ulceby.

REEVE, John. Served on Grand Jury at the trial of Lucy Ann Buxton, at the Lincoln Assizes. Resident of Leadenham House.

RICHTER, Reverend Henry William. Chaplain of Lincoln Castle Prison and Rector of St Paul in the Bail, Lincoln. Resident of 23 Minster Yard, Lincoln.

RUDGARD, William. Presiding magistrate with J R Battle at initial hearing of Lucy Ann Buxton for theft. Resident of Newland House, Lincoln.

SHUTTLEWORTH, Joseph. Manufacturer of Agricultural Machinery at Stamp End Works, Lincoln. Served on Grand Jury at the trial of Lucy Ann Buxton, at the Lincoln Assizes. Resident at New Road, Lincoln.

SMITH, Horace. Counsel for the Prosecution at the trial of Lucy Ann Buxton, at the Lincoln Assizes.

THORPE, James. Gave evidence at inquest into the death of John Edward Buxton and at the trial of Lucy Ann Buxton, at the Lincoln Assizes. Resident of Metheringham.

VERNON, Honourable Gowran Charles. Presiding judge, Lincoln Quarter Sessions, at trial of Lucy Ann Buxton for robbery from the house of George Hardy.

WRIGHT, Samuel Wright. Served on Grand Jury at the trial of Lucy Ann Buxton, at the Lincoln Assizes.

Chapter Two

Emma Wade (1860-?)

Emma Wade: Timeline

1860: Birth of Emma Wade, daughter of Ann and William Wade of Stamford.

11th June, 1862: Emma Wade baptised at All Saints' Church, Stamford.

1874-1877: domestic servant in the employment of William Dalton, corn merchant, and his wife, Sophia Dalton, resident of The Grange, Morton, near Bourne.

Friday, 18th April, 1879: attempted suicide of Emma Wade and death of Constance Mary Scarcliffe Wade, aged five months, daughter of Emma Wade and Henry Scarcliffe, in Stamford.

Monday, 21st April, 1879: inquest at Stamford Town Hall into the death of Constance Mary Scarcliffe Wade, before Coroner James Edward Atter: adjourned.

Tuesday, 22nd April, 1879: burial of Constance Mary Scarcliffe Wade.

Thursday, 24th April, 1879: resumed inquest into the death of Constance Mary Scarcliffe Wade at Stamford Town Hall: coroner's jury finds Emma Wade guilty of wilful murder.

Saturday, 26th April, 1879: Emma Wade appears before magistrates in Stamford, charged with the wilful murder of Constance Mary Scarcliffe Wade. Remanded in custody at the house of her parents in Stamford, on account of her poor health.

Monday, 28th April, 1879: further hearing in front of the magistrates. Emma Wade committed to Lincoln Assizes on a capital charge.

Tuesday, 29th April, 1879: received into Lincoln County prison at 9 o'clock in the morning.

Wednesday, 30th April, 1879: trial of Emma Wade for wilful murder at the Nottinghamshire and Lincolnshire Assizes, in Lincoln, in front of Mr Justice Robert Lush. Jury finds her guilty of wilful murder, but with a strong recommendation for mercy.

Wednesday, 7th May, 1879: letter to the Mayor of Stamford from Sir John Charles Dalrymple Hay to inform him of the decision of the Home Secretary to reprieve Emme Wade, with enclosed letter from Whitehall, signed by Sir Adolphus A F O Liddell, confirming the Home Secretary's decision.

Thursday, 8th May, 1879: Major Edward Mackay, Governor of Lincoln County prison, receives telegram from the Home Secretary, confirming the reprieve of Emma Wade, commuting her sentence to one year in prison with hard labour.

Tuesday, 22nd April, 1880: discharged from Lincoln County prison.

1881: employed as a domestic servant by Henry Hawkins, hairdresser, and his wife, Elizabeth, resident at Church Street, Market Deeping.

'The Staple of a Thousand Fictions': the condemnation and reprieve of Emma Wade

On the afternoon of Friday, 18th April, 1868, nineteen year old Emma Wade, living with her parents at 1 Palmer's Building in Stamford, wrote a letter to Mr Henry Scarcliffe, the father of her illegitimate infant daughter, which Louisa Wade, her elder sister, kindly posted for her around 3 o'clock. The letter only had to travel a short distance across town and so arrived by early evening at 23 Broad Street, the home of the addressee.

The letter was quite remarkable in many respects.

It was written by a young woman in the middle of a distressing personal crisis and yet the prose has a degree of poise, polish and control. Despite the disturbing subject matter, in which the writer announced that she was intending to commit suicide and quite possibly to kill her infant daughter, the feelings expressed range between calm reflection, unruffled disappointment and the flat acceptance of a sombre inevitability. Sections of the letter are both emotive and emotional, hinting at underlying distress. The turbulent feelings which gave rise to the writing of the letter in the first place, however, are contained and restrained. In addition, the style of the letter, artfully using a repeated plaintive refrain at critical junctures, suggests a piece of writing carefully constructed in tranquillity, rather than one scribbled in the heat of the moment.

Whether the intention of the letter was to leave behind a justification for her proposed rash course of action or to exert some kind of pressure on Henry Scarcliffe is not clear. What is certain, however, is that the letter became a key piece of evidence in the trial of Emma Wade, charged with having poisoned her five months old daughter, Constance Mary Scarcliffe Wade, with strychnine, on the evening of Friday, 18th April, 1879, and who was sentenced to be hanged in Lincoln less than three weeks later.

Inquest into the death of Constance Mary Scarcliffe Wade, Stamford Town Hall, before Coroner James Edward Atter, Monday 21st April, 1879

The report of the inquest in the *Stamford Mercury*, with the strapline 'Infanticide and Attempted Suicide', was published on 25th April. The account was preceded by a detailed paragraph which provided the reader with essential background information to the sensational local story, some of which was not entirely accurate.

The 'distressing case of child murder and infanticide' involved the daughter of Police Constable William Wade, who was a familiar figure in the town. According to the report, Emma Wade had poisoned her illegitimate child 'in a fit of despondency' with *Battle's Vermin Killer* and had attempted to take her own life with a dose of the same substance. Her cries of pain had been heard by her mother and sister, who had quickly administered salt and water, mustard and water and other emetics. The life of Emma Wade was saved, but her infant child died about an hour 'after severe suffering'.

The formal inquest into the death of Constance Mary Scarcliffe Wade was held at the Stamford Town Hall in front of local solicitor and coroner, Mr James Edward Atter.

The first witness to testify was a friend and near neighbour of Emma Wade, Mrs Fanny Weatherington. On Thursday, 17th April, she had taken tea with Emma Wade, who had visited her that afternoon; the infant child, at that point, appeared to be in a good state of health. The following day, around 7 o'clock in the evening, she had been called to the Wade house and had discovered Emma Wade sitting on the side of her bed crying. On enquiring as to what was the matter, Emma Wade had cried out, 'Oh, go and see my baby, it is dying'.

Having not been given a clear picture as to what was happening by Emma Wade, Mrs Weatherington asked her sister Louisa, who was holding the baby, to throw some light on the matter. Louisa Wade revealed that her sister had taken poison and had given some to the baby.

At this point, the level-headed Mrs Weatherington,

took charge of the fraught situation, directing Louisa Wade to take the baby downstairs and give her something to make her sick, whilst she gave Emma Wade salt and water plus mustard and water to similarly make her sick.

After having administered the emetics, she went downstairs to attend to the baby, who by now was convulsing and frothing at the mouth; in addition, her body was rigid and her hands clenched.

In due course, Dr Greenwood, the local surgeon, arrived and he immediately ordered the baby to be placed in a warm bath; he also entrusted Mrs Weatherington to administer 'some powder in hot water' to the sick child.

By now, Emma Wade was totally distraught, constantly exclaiming, 'Oh my baby is dead, my baby is dead!' Mrs Weatherington commented that 'she appeared to suffer intense grief, as well as bodily pain'.

Constance died in the arms of the witness, at some time between 8 and 9 o'clock, although Emma Wade had been unable to say what she had given to the child. This was resolved by Louisa Wade who found paper wrappers which contained *Battle's Vermin Killer* powder in the bedroom.

Mrs Weatherington concluded her helpful testimony by recalling that Emma Wade had seemed very unhappy on the Thursday afternoon, on account of her having 'had some words with her mother'.

William J Swann, apprentice to the Stamford chemist and druggist, Frederick Dickinson, presented a very familiar deposition, heard in many similar cases, which related to the sale of poison to an individual who was later suspected of murder. Emma Wade had purchased a threepenny packet of *Battle's Vermin Killer* on the morning of Friday, 18th April, claiming that it was intended to kill mice.

Thomas Porter Greenwood, physician and surgeon, told the coroner's court that he had been summoned by PC Wade at about 7 o'clock in the evening and had found both Emma Wade and her child suffering from the symptoms of strychnine poisoning. He had immediately directed that the baby be placed in a hot bath, whilst he attended to the mother with emetics - an account which was slightly at variance with the testimony of Mrs Weatherington. He did confirm, however, that he had asked Mrs Weatherington to give the infant an emetic, but he thought that she had not swallowed it as her jaw was made rigid by the poison. He had left the house to retrieve 'some other remedy', but on his return, about fifteen minutes later, the infant had died.

Emma Wade was very sick at the time, but he thought that she was now likely to recover. She had told him that she had taken some *Battle's Vermin Killer* and had given a small amount to her infant daughter.

Both he and Dr William Newman had made a post mortem examination of the body of the child and had preserved the stomach for analysis. He confirmed that it would only require one sixteenth of a grain of strychnine to kill a small child.

Henry Scarcliffe, assistant to Stamford jeweller, Henry Norton, confirmed that he had received a letter 'in the handwriting of Emma Wade' by post, dated Friday, 18th April. After reading it, he had handed it over to the police.

The letter was read out in court and transcribed by the reporter, probably mistaking the word 'heavy' for 'heaving'.

Dear Harry – I am sorry to write to you. I return your portrait with heaving heart. It is sadder than I can express to anyone; but I have borne my mother's treatment until I can do so no longer. It is all because my father will not turn me out in the street. The words she uttered about me and baby are too cruel to express to you. Dear Harry, I love my child as I love my life, but I cannot go through the treatment I am undergoing. Now my life is a complete misery, and my child too. Dear Harry, I wish to bid you farewell in this world, but hope to meet you in another, never to part again. I hope the Lord will forgive me and take me to a home of rest. Harry, I have one comfort, and that is I know my child will be happy. So now, dear Harry, you must put me out of your mind, and look for something brighter. Dear Harry, I wish to tell you it is nothing on your part. My love has never vanished. I love you now as I loved you at first. You have been in my thoughts from morning to night. So now must bid you farewell for ever. I hope you enjoy happiness in this world and the next. My heart is too full to speak all: so goodbye for ever (kisses). I have sent you a piece of baby's hair. You won't forget her name, Constance Mary Scarcliffe.

Henry Scarcliffe, father of the child, continued his deposition by assuring the court that he had made financial provision for the child at the office of Mr Atter. Perhaps more significantly in terms of understanding the sorry events, he had seen Emma Wade on the previous Tuesday night and she 'seemed very unhappy and very wild in her conversation'. However, she had not threatened to 'do anything to herself'. He had asked what had upset her so much and was told that it was 'her mother's ill-treatment'.

Being an elder sister of Emma Wade and having been closely involved in the events of Friday, 18th April, the deposition of Louisa Wade was an important one.

She testified that at around 7 o'clock on the Friday night she heard screams from her sister, who had been upstairs for about twenty minutes. Her mother had instructed her to go upstairs to investigate the matter. She discovered her sister lying on the bed with the baby by her side. Emma Wade had said to her sister, 'Oh Louisa, take the baby, for I have poisoned it myself'.

She immediately ran downstairs with the baby, sat close to the fire and gave her salt water to make her sick, whilst her mother attended to Emma. Her father, who was in bed, got up and went for the doctor. She nursed the child until Dr Greenwood arrived at the house.

Perhaps surprisingly, in light of the letter and the deposition of Henry Scarcliffe, Louisa Wade said that she had never heard her mother say anything cruel to her sister, nor upbraid her. What she did say was that on the Thursday her mother had wished Emma to 'put the child out to nurse and go back to a situation'. The response of her sister had been to refuse to go back into service and she had declared that she was 'very unhappy, and could not stand it much longer'.

At this point, the coroner halted the proceedings and ordered an adjournment until Thursday, 24th April.

Sergeant George Dalrymple was ordered by Mr Atter to take the contents of the deceased's stomach to Lincoln for chemical analysis. He further ordered that Superintendent Richard Ward should ensure the safe and secure custody of Emma Wade. This part of the report ended with the information that the

Stamford solicitor, Daniel Evans, had observed the proceedings on her behalf, as Emma Wade had been too ill to attend the inquest.

Resumed inquest into the death of Constance Mary Scarcliffe Wade, Stamford Town Hall, before Coroner James Edward Atter, Monday 21st April, 1879

Due to the quick turnaround between the initial inquest and its resumption at 12 o'clock, on 24th April, the *Stamford Mercury* was able to report on both in its publication of Friday, 25th April.

Emma Wade was in court for the resumption of the case, having been brought to the Town Hall from her father's house in 'a closed fly'. The reporter observed sympathetically that Emma Wade 'appeared very much depressed and very ill and weak', and that she had to be assisted from the carriage into the court, where she was once again represented by Daniel Evans with a watching brief.

Only two further depositions were heard: the first from Sergeant Dalrymple, who confirmed the routine information that he had done his duty in delivering the sealed jars containing the deceased child's stomach to Lincoln; the second from Dr George May Lowe, the Lincolnshire County Analyst, who presented his findings to the court.

Dr Lowe reported that the stomach of the child had contained two ounces of a light-coloured fluid and that the lining membrane, whilst pale, was in a healthy condition. An examination of the fluid under the microscope had revealed the presence of flour, starch, milk, and a small fragment of bacon or ham. More importantly, it also contained a few particles of Prussian blue. On submitting the contents of the stomach to chemical analysis, he discovered about three quarters of a grain of strychnine, which would have been quite sufficient to kill a five month old child. Prussian blue, he added, was used as a colouring agent in *Battle's Vermin Killer*.

The jury took thirty minutes of private discussion to reach a verdict of wilful murder against Emma Wade.

She was then taken back home to be in the custody of her father until she 'was in a fit condition to be present at the borough magistrates'.

Hearing before magistrates at the Stamford Petty Sessions, Saturday 26th April, 1879, concerning the wilful murder of Constance Mary Scarcliffe by Emma Wade

The *Stamford Mercury*, 2nd May, began its report with a description of Emma Wade in a reduced and pathetic state, arriving at the Petty Sessions, held at the Town Hall,. She 'still appeared very ill' and 'had to be supported during the whole of the proceedings'; further, 'her mental suffering seemed to be exceedingly great'.

Before recording the depositions of the witnesses, the newspaper noted the absence of Emma Wade's solicitor, William Farmery Law, who was 'out of town' - which seemed an unfortunate dereliction of professional duty.

The deposition of Louisa Wade repeated the narrative of the troubling events of Friday, 18th April, on the whole, although it did include additional material not heard or reported from the inquest. It included the new domestic details of her waiting for her mother to finish writing a letter to take to the post, when she heard the screams of her sister coming from upstairs; and that she had discovered the wrappers of *Battle's Vermin Killer* in her sister's box. It also included a good deal of insistence that Emma Wade was very attached to her child: she used to appear 'very fond of it' and she had never heard her 'threaten to destroy the child': nor had she any reason 'to think she would do anything to it'. She also deposed that her sister 'had been in very low spirits ever since I have been at home'.

Mrs Fanny Weatherington, wife of local sawyer, Henry Weatherington, recounted her deposition heard at the inquest, adding that she had helped Emma Wade to undress and get into bed. She also emphasised, using words very similar to those of Louisa Wade, that she had never heard Emma Wade 'threaten to destroy her child' and that she was 'always fond of it'. Mrs Weatherington also observed that Emma Wade had been 'very unhappy ever since the child was born' and 'has not appeared herself at times'.

Interestingly, she was questioned by PC Wade, who seemed to focus upon the part played by his wife in the unfolding drama. Mrs Weatherington told him that Emma had been at her house on the Thursday when she learnt about 'words at home with her mother' which had caused her to 'appear very much distressed'. She denied that Emma had told her that her mother had threatened to leave the house as a result of their differences; but qualified this statement by claiming that she had heard Mrs Wade say as much at some point in the past

The appearance of William Swann, the apprentice who sold the poison to Emma Wade, added nothing new to his evidence at the inquest.

Dr Greenwood repeated his deposition from the inquest concerning his initial attendance at the Wade house, although he changed it slightly, when he told the court that he had tried to give the infant an emetic, as opposed to Mrs Weatherington having been given the responsibility. He also expanded his account of the post mortem he had carried out with

Dr Newman, noting that the membranes of the brain indicated convulsions before death, but cautioned that such convulsions might arise from causes other than poisoning.

He ended his deposition by verifying that he had witnessed Louisa Wade searching through the box of her sister and finding the papers used to wrap *Battle's Vermin Killer*. The papers in question were held up for the benefit of the court.

The testimony of Henry Scarcliffe, however, was a totally different matter, and contributed a good deal more to an understanding of his relationship with Emma Wade, and also with her parents.

He confirmed, rather coyly, that he had 'kept company with the deceased', but openly stated that he was the father of the child, which had been born five months ago. Since her confinement, Mr Scarcliffe had only seen Emma Wade occasionally, although he was with her on the evening of 15th April. He deposed once again that Emma Wade's state of mind was volatile, describing her being 'very much excited'. He also expanded upon the issue of Emma Wade's conflict with her mother as a source of great unhappiness. She complained to Henry Scarcliffe about her mother's 'ill-treatment' of her, who had 'called her disgracefully on account of the child'. However, even though she appeared to be very unhappy, he insisted that she did not say anything which might have led him to think she would do what she had done.

Mr Scarcliffe confirmed that he had received a letter in the evening post from Emma and he also assured the court that he had immediately set out to go and see the accused after reading it. On the way to the house, he had met with Elizabeth Wade, who told him what had happened, and so he turned back home.

Once again, PC William Wade was given the opportunity to question a witness. The questioning by Emma Wade's father created a sense that Mr and Mrs Wade did not entirely approve of their nineteen year old daughter's relationship with the twenty-six year old Mr Scarcliffe. His first question was whether his daughter had ever told him 'that her father and mother wished the acquaintance broken off?' Henry Scarcliffe's monosyllabic response was an unambiguous: 'yes'. The second question, similarly tried to establish clarity concerning William Wade's paternal entitlements, using a tricky double-negative: 'Have I not wished you not to come after her?' The laconic response of 'Not since her confinement' may have prompted a degree of speculation in the courtroom concerning domestic difficulties for Emma Wade in her relationship with Henry Scarcliffe.

After Sergeant Dalrymple confirmed that the consigning of the medical evidence had been properly carried out, the Bench halted proceedings by asking Dr Greenwood whether or not it was safe to remove the prisoner to Lincoln. Dr Greenwood pointed out that she was still very weak and that it would be prudent for her to remain in Stamford for a few days.

After a short consultation in private, the magistrates remanded Emma Wade until Monday, 28th April. According to the newspaper, Emma Wade left the court 'crying bitterly'.

Resumed hearing before magistrates at the Stamford Petty Sessions, Saturday 26th April, 1879, concerning the wilful murder of Constance Mary Scarcliffe by Emma Wade

If the description of the entry of Emma Wade into court on 26th April did not produce a sympathetic response from the reader of the *Stamford Mercury*, the report of her reappearance, two days later, would have perhaps succeeded. She was again conveyed to the Town Hall in a closed carriage to protect her from any curious sightseers. Once out of the carriage, such was her condition, she had to be supported on the arms of two female friends, as she 'uttered piteous cries'.

After his brief flirtation with sentiment, the reporter became more matter of fact, noting that Mr Evans had appeared on the prisoner's behalf and that the newspaper would only be appending 'the more interesting evidence'.

What followed was a miscellany of statements made by Louisa Wade, Fanny Weatherington, Dr Greenwood and Henry Scarcliffe, and the repetition by Dr Lowe of his medical investigations. Most of the witness statements, possibly made under cross-examination from Mr Evans, reinforced the narrative of Emma Wade having been persecuted by her mother and created an image of her as having been a very unhappy young woman.

Louisa Wade's deposition seemed a good deal more forthright than on previous occasions, presenting her mother as a much more unpleasant and overbearing figure than before. She had heard her mother objecting to Emma staying at home, and that she had told her several times that she must put the baby out to a nurse and find herself a job. She had last heard this kind of conversation on the afternoon of Thursday, 17th April.

Fanny Weatherington, who had spoken to Emma Wade on the same day, was called straight after Louisa Wade, and confirmed the same narrative of domestic conflict between daughter and mother.

Dr Greenwood was re-sworn and told the court that Emma Wade was 'in extreme danger' when he first saw her and that without his medical intervention, she would have died. Rather than being presented with an opportunity to advertise his professional competence, the doctor was probably being prompted to confirm that Emma Wade's suicide attempt had been a serious one and, by implication, that it was driven by her mother's unkindness towards her and the baby.

Henry Scarcliffe's account of the domestic difficulties, like that of Louisa Wade, was an intensified version of his previously reported deposition. He emphasised, once again, that when he last saw Emma she was 'excited and appeared to be unhappy', but he also said that 'the prisoner complained to me of the bad treatment of her mother *many times*'.

Once Dr Lowe had repeated his medical analysis, the hearing was complete: Emma Wade was committed for trial on a capital charge and removed to Lincoln on Tuesday, 29th April.

As a postscript to the resumed hearing, the newspaper informed the interested reader that during the course of the afternoon, Emma Wade 'fainted and appeared quite prostrated'.

Because there were only a few days between the resumed hearing in front of the magistrates in Stamford and the trial in Lincoln, the *Stamford Mercury* was able to report on both in one issue. Without even a hint of a spoiler alert, the end of the report on the resumed hearing directed its readers to the report of the trial on a different page, which had resulted in a death sentence being passed, but with a recommendation for mercy by the jury.

The newspaper was confident that 'the extreme punishment will not be carried out'. In addition, it reported that events had moved so fast that a memorial petition was already being organised on her behalf for submission to the Home Secretary, and the newspaper thought that it would be 'numerously signed, there being a strong feeling of sympathy in the town on her behalf'.

Trial of Emma Wade before Justice Robert Lush at the Lincoln Assizes, charged with the wilful murder of Constance Mary Scarcliffe Wade, Wednesday 30th April, 1879

Whilst Emma Wade was having to endure listening to the painful reminders of the events of Friday, 18th April, seated in Stamford Town Hall, close to the man to whom she had recently sent a suicide letter ironically predicting a happy reunion with him in a future life, Justice Robert Lush, just over fifty miles away and unquestionably rooted in the present life, arrived in Lincoln to preside over the administration of justice.

The *Market Rasen Weekly Mail and Lincolnshire Advertiser*, published 3rd May, recorded the civic reception of his Lordship in the city in some detail and had clearly been impressed by the ceremonial grandeur of the occasion.

He had arrived at the Midland station on Monday, 28th April, at 3.18, and was met by the High Sheriff of Lincolnshire, the Honourable E G Finch Hatton and his Chaplain; the Acting Under-Sheriff, Mr A B Burton; and the City Sheriff, Mr Henry Pratt and his Under-Sheriff, Mr J G Williams. From the station, he was taken in the High-Sheriff's carriage, escorted by javelin men and city constables, to be received by the Mayor and other dignitaries at the City Sessions House, where he opened the Commission for the City. He then moved on to the County Hall to open the Commission for the County and was later to attend Divine Service at the Cathedral.

The spectacle and, in particular, the High Sheriff's carriage 'were greatly admired' - the introduction of a couple of outriders 'lending a novel and striking feature to the display'.

What was not so novel and certainly less pleasing on the eye was the list of prisoners, mainly from Nottingham, charged with various offences, ranging from petty theft to murder.

At 10 o'clock, on Tuesday, 29th April, Justice Lush began the earnest business of swearing in the Grand Jury, as well as the city jury, before addressing them with his reflections on recent organisational changes and the Calendar of cases to be considered.

By the time he had completed his deliberations, mainly related to 'a very serious and painful case' of a young woman accused of murdering her child, Emma Wade had made her journey from Stamford. She had been received into the Lincoln County prison at 9 o'clock that morning, her identity registered and recorded as Female Prisoner Number 20, with a fresh complexion, brown hair, hazel eyes, round face and of medium build, possessing only imperfect skills in reading and writing.

The Grand Jury sworn in for the trial of Emma Wade was an experienced one, six of whom had served at the trial of Lucy Ann Buxton, also in front of Justice Lush. It consisted of:

Sir John Thorald (Foreman)
H C Allenby
Sir Charles Anderson
Richard Charles Bergne-Coupland
L Burton
W R Emeris
J Ferraby
John Lewis Ffytche
Thomas Garfit
B R Langton
Thomas Charles John Moore
C F M Mundy
R H C Nevil(e)

C J B Parker
William Parker (Jr)
John Reeve
Charles Sibthorp
Montague Richard Waldo Sibthorp
William Henry Smyth(e)
Robert J Taylor
Charles Thorald
Samuel Wright Wright

Justice Lush for the most part seemed either unconcerned or unsurprised at the cases sent over from Nottingham, which he described as being 'of an ordinary character', requiring no comment from him: perhaps the felons in question, two of whom came close to being flogged as well as being sentenced to fifteen months hard labour for assault and robbery, might have taken issue with the apparently blasé indifference of the judge to their troubled existence.

The case of child murder had only just come in and therefore did not appear on the Calendar. For the benefit of the jury, Justice Lush reviewed some of the main facets of the case, highlighting a good deal of unhappiness in the accused's home and that she had admitted to her sister that she had poisoned her own child, as well as attempting to kill herself. He also mentioned that he had been informed that such was the state of the accused's health that it was 'probable that she would not take her trial there'. However, the evidence was available and a bill would be presented to the jury, which 'would not give them any trouble'.

The report of the trial in the *Stamford Mercury* was a long one, but was interrupted by a reference to the exposition of the case against the accused being available for perusal in a previous page of the newspaper.

The Counsel for the Prosecution was Mr Etherington Smith and for the Defence, Mr Marston Clarke Buszard, both of them formidable performers in a courtroom. In a sense, the choice of Mr Buszard to defend Emma Wade was a natural one, having strong political connections with Stamford, the town which he would represent as a Liberal Member of Parliament the following year.

The opening address of the Prosecution was surprisingly low-key, in which Mr Smith told the jury that their verdict would simply rest upon two questions: was the poison which caused the death of the infant administered by the accused and did she have in her mind, at the time, the intention to kill the child? Employing a well-worn rhetorical strategy, he presented himself as an eminently reasonable man who did not stand before them to express a personal opinion on the case nor to prejudice the jury against the accused. However, he felt compelled to observe that the purchase of the vermin killer powder and the letter written to the father of the child strongly suggested that the accused did have an intention to commit murder.

Having planted the idea of intent, Etherington Smith very quickly, very reasonably and somewhat disingenuously, reassured the jury that if after hearing all the evidence it 'could conscientiously come to the conclusion that she had not in her mind any such intention, he should be only too glad' to hear a verdict of Not Guilty.

If reported fully and correctly, it was not Mr Smith's most persuasive performance as a prosecuting counsel. The hard work was left to Mr Buszard, who was faced with the problem of explaining away some very compelling circumstantial evidence against the accused.

In his address to the jury, he opened with an apology, explaining that he had been called upon to undertake the case involving 'the greatest issue which could be decided in a court' at very short notice. His apology might have been seen as a transparent rhetorical ploy, but given both the extension and compression of the processes leading to the trial, which had involved two adjournments, as well as the uncertainty surrounding the attendance of Emma Wade in Lincoln, it may well have been true. In addition, the reluctance of Stamford solicitors to undertake trials in Lincoln due to the inconvenience and low rates of payment, discussed at the meeting of the Stamford Estate & Watch Committee, 21st April, suggested potential administrative difficulties.

From the outset, it was clear that the Defence intended to conduct his case, at least in part, on an emotive level. He had been involved in many cases similar to the present one, he said, but 'none had been sadder than the one the jury had then to decide'. In reminding the jury of their duty to come to a decision on the issue of wilful murder, he referred to Emma Wade as 'the poor girl', rather than the accused or the prisoner. That the 'poor girl', in fear for her life and recovering from strychnine poisoning, was sitting in full view of the jury in a state of some distress, would certainly have been a helpful prop to support the strategy.

Mr Buszard did not wish to dwell upon the dreadful consequences of a Guilty verdict, as the jury were only too well aware of the responsibility which rested upon their shoulders. But what he did wish to point out to the jury was that 'the poor creature's life had been entrusted to his keeping' and that he 'felt utterly inadequate to discharge the duty which devolved upon him'. A pained and humble confession of personal inadequacy, on top of having had little time to prepare the case, was a perhaps deliberate contrast with his description of a confident Counsel for the Prosecution who had insisted 'over and over again' that the accused intended to kill the child and was therefore guilty of wilful murder.

Before presenting his arguments for finding Emma Wade Not Guilty, Mr Buszard accepted the fact that the jury might arrive at a Guilty verdict. Significantly, his polite acceptance of the fact was not framed in terms of being convinced by the evidence, but rather of not being able to find 'feelings of compassion' in favour of his client. The binary opposites of subjective feeling and objective facts were taken up by Lord Justice Lush in his summary of the case and also became the subject of some uneasy analysis by contemporary commentators on the case.

Probably drawing upon his experience or knowledge of other cases of child murder, Mr Buszard pointed out that this was not an issue of an overburdened mother who wished to get rid of her child; nor was it a case of a father refusing to provide support for a child, so that it 'hung round her neck' and prevented her 'getting on in life'. On the contrary, Emma Wade was a 'fond and devoted mother' and the father had 'provided for the sustenance of the child'.

As far as he knew, the 'young girl' had never complained about her child and it had been well-received into the family. The only thing that she did complain about was her mother's conduct towards her, having been pressed to go back into service, rather than 'live on the family'. These facts quite clearly removed any possible motive for the alleged crime and these facts should be the starting point for the jury's thinking, the Counsel for the Defence suggested.

Further, the evidence did not establish that 'the girl' had administered poison to the child, 'knowing full well what she was doing'. Before the jury could arrive at 'the terrible verdict', it was incumbent upon the Counsel for the Prosecution to satisfy them beyond all reasonable doubt that she had administered the poison with the intention of murdering the child and was fully aware of the consequences of her actions.

The report ended with the Defence Counsel's apparently cursory analysis of the letter sent by Emma Wade to Henry Scarcliffe, merely asserting that rather than proving the case against the prisoner it contradicted it, as did the other facts of the case. His conclusion was the theory that the mother, after taking poison herself 'gave a little to the child, not knowing in her agony what she was doing.'

The report in the *Stamford Mercury* gave the impression that the defence of Emma Wade fizzled out with a lame excuse and without having properly examined the letter. The coverage of the trial in the *Lincolnshire Chronicle*, published on the same day, however, reported this part of the proceedings in much greater detail, and showed that Mr Buszard had very carefully analysed the contents of the letter to support his arguments.

The summing up by Justice Robert Lush reported in the *Stamford Mercury* suggested that he was aware both of the highly emotive nature of the case and also of the Defence Counsel having made effective use of it. He cautioned the jury that whatever his or their feelings, they must do their duty and be guided by the evidence.

It was clear to Robert Lush that the evidence heard in court against Emma Wade pointed to her having administered poison to her own child. The Defence Counsel had not made any reference to the possibility of her being of 'unsound mind' nor that she was 'labouring under temporary insanity'; neither had there been any suggestion of provocation. In which case, the jury could not reach a verdict of manslaughter, only of wilful murder.

Whilst acknowledging that the father had acted in a kindly manner towards the child and that the prisoner had been adversely affected by an argument with her mother, he reminded the jury that she had told both Dr Greenwood and her sister that she had taken some *Battle's Vermin Killer* and had also given some of the powder to the child.

These were incontrovertible facts, but the letter in which she had stated her intention to commit suicide was ambiguous in its declarations relating to the infant. The crux cited by his Lordship, 'I know that my child will be happy', may have implied that she intended to kill herself and leave the child behind. In which case, the poison must have got into the stomach of the child inadvertently and therefore the verdict of the jury must be manslaughter.

The jury took an hour to reach its decision of Guilty, but with a strong recommendation of mercy.

According to the report, Emma Wade appeared to be 'in a state of stupor' throughout the trial and remained 'perfectly passive' as the sentence was being passed, after which she had to be carried out of court.

The version of the trial narrated by the *Lincolnshire Chronicle* of 2nd May, 1879, included the witness statements, as well as the addresses of the learned counsels to the court and the summary of Justice Lush. In all three areas, the Lincoln newspaper provided interesting material not included in the *Stamford Mercury*.

The preamble to the account of the trial was a sympathetic one in its depiction of Emma Wade in the courtroom. She 'appeared to be very weak and in a prostrate state' and was accommodated in a seat throughout the proceedings. On being called upon to plead, she was only able to speak 'in a faint and almost inaudible voice'.

Interestingly, it noted that she had requested to be tried at the Lincoln Assizes, despite only having been committed 'on the grave charge' on the previous Monday.

The opening address by Mr Etherington Smith produced two new pieces of information, one of which could have been used to advantage by an aggressive Counsel for the Prosecution, but wasn't. First, the court was informed that Emma Wade had been living at home for the previous nine months and had been helping her mother with the housework. The second piece of information, mentioned almost carelessly, was that the mother had a large family at the time, although no details were provided.

Census returns and other official documents reveal that between 1851 and 1883, Ann Wade, the mother of Emma, had fourteen children with William Wade. In the 1861 Census, there were seven children, aged between one and ten years of age; in the 1871 Census, there were nine children, aged between one and seventeen years of age; and in the 1881 Census, there were still seven children living at home, aged between six and nineteen years of age. In 1879, the year of the alleged murder, it is clear that Emma Wade and her child would have been an economic pressure on such a large family, and an obvious mitigating context for the apparently harsh demand from Ann Wade that her daughter should go back into service in order to ease that pressure.

Mr Smith accepted that the mother of the prisoner

may have spoken harshly to her about the child and that Emma Wade 'seemed to be very much depressed and low-spirited indeed'. The follow up to these sympathetic concessions, however, made it clear that he was more interested in drawing attention to the purchase of *Battle's Vermin Killer* on the morning of Friday, 18th April, than in any unpleasant domestic disputes.

In an extended version of the report found in the *Stamford Mercury*, Mr Smith described the prisoner having gone to the chemist's shop to purchase the poison which had killed the child. The assistant 'knew her perfectly well and there was nothing suspicious in her manner'. She had told him that the poison was required to deal with mice and she had signed the book 'kept for registering the sale of poisons'. The image of the prisoner constructed by Mr Etherington Smith, rather than one of a young woman in low spirits, was a quite different one of a young woman involved in a calculated act of deception in order to facilitate an act of suicide and child murder.

The point was reinforced by the Counsel for the Prosecution when he referred to the letter written by Emma Wade, theatrically producing it in court for all to see as the clinching evidence of intent to kill.

The reported depositions of both Louisa Wade and Fanny Weatherington affirmed their views of

Emma Wade as a victim of her mother, low spirits and circumstance.

Under cross-examination by Mr Buszard concerning the arguments between Emma Wade and her mother, Louisa confirmed that her sister 'always seemed very unhappy and low-spirited' during her time at home. She also produced a version of a mother who not only pressed her daughter to go back into service, but also 'urged her to go, sometimes rather harshly so, telling her to get out of the house and go and get a place'. The day before the 'occurrence', there had been harsh words spoken which Emma 'felt very much'. Emma had often said that she could not bear her mother's conduct towards her and 'that was the state of mind Emma was in down to the time that this happened'.

It was a harrowing testimony and, at the same time, a very interesting one as the culmination of a pattern of increasingly hostile narratives about the mother: at the inquest, her deposition was a restrained one of never having witnessed her mother rebuking her sister, which shifted at the magistrate's hearing to a less cautious account of relations between the two in which Mrs Wade pressed her daughter to find employment, and now culminated at the Assize trial in the suggestion of veiled threats to evict Emma.

The deposition of Louisa Wade, as reported in the *Lincolnshire Chronicle*, also included a graphic description of Emma Wade after having swallowed a quantity of *Battle's Vermin Killer*. She had discovered her sister lying on the bed 'rubbing her head very much' and she had 'moved about the bed very much, as if in great pain'.

It was a distressing image of the young woman confirmed by Mrs Weatherington when she gave her account: Emma Wade was enduring 'great pain of body' and was 'in very great agony'. Under cross-examination from the Counsel for the Defence, Fanny Weatherington also confirmed that her friend had also endured 'great distress of mind' about the baby, 'crying out about it, and anxious that something could be done for it'.

The deposition of William Swann, the shop apprentice who had sold the poison to Emma Wade, confirmed, word for word, the remarks of the Counsel for the Defence, but also included the additional information that the transaction took place at 11 o'clock.

Under cross-examination from Mr Buszard, Dr Greenwood deposed that the body of the deceased child was well-nourished and that he had found Emma Wade 'in great distress, both in mind and body'. In essence, the description of Emma Wade's condition was similar to that heard from Dr Greenwood before the magistrates, except that the language used in the first deposition, speaking of her being 'in grave danger' was arguably less subjective than her being greatly distressed in mind and body. It certainly corroborated the untrained observations of both Louisa Wade and Fanny Weatherington.

After giving his report Dr Lowe, the county analyst, was questioned by both the Justice Lush and Mr Etherington Smith, but the questions, relating to the poison, its strength and the means of detection, seemed more like an exercise in polite interest, rather than a serious pressing for information.

The cross-examination of Henry Scarcliffe by both counsels and the judge seemed much more to the point.

In response to Mr Etherington Smith, he deposed that he had received the letter from Emma Wade at seven-thirty in the evening and had set off to the Wade house immediately, but had been stopped by Elizabeth Wade, who had told him what had taken place.

In response to Justice Lush, Henry Scarcliffe confirmed that the handwriting on the envelope was that of Emma Wade. The only additional information from his earlier testimony in Stamford was that he had handed over the letter to Sergeant Dalrymple.

At this point, the Clerk of the Arraigns, Arthur Duke Coleridge, read the letter out to the court.

Henry Scarcliffe was also cross-examined by Mr Buszard, confirming that he was the father of the deceased child and that he had met with Emma Wade on Tuesday, 15th April. Once again, he deposed that she 'appeared to be in distress and low-spirited' and once again, he said that Emma complained about her mother. What was startling and explicitly went beyond anything said before, either by Scarcliffe or the other witnesses sympathetic to the accused, was that her mother had wanted her to leave, not just the house, but Stamford altogether.

Before reporting the closing address of the Learned Counsels, the newspaper recorded that Mr Etherington Smith referred to the father of Emma Wade, who had appeared at the magistrate's court in Stamford: he did not intend to call him 'unless the court desired it'. It was an interesting decision, but a regrettable one from the point of view of the public gallery and the newspaper readers who had been following the case. On a human level of domestic politics, William Wade was very much at the heart of the matter, with allegiances towards both his wife and his children, but with an antipathy towards Henry Scarcliffe. On a legal level, he was in a position to verify, modify or deny the train of events witnessed on Friday, 18th April at his house by others.

The closing address by the Counsel for the Defence was reported more precisely and extensively than in the *Stamford Mercury* and confirmed that Mr Buszard, in the face of strong circumstantial evidence, constructed a credible defence rather than merely asserting vague claims leading to an improbable fiction. The opening of the address, inevitably, emphasised the sadness of the case.

The construction of the argument for a Not Guilty verdict followed some predictable lines of argument, such as Emma Wade being a 'fond loving mother', based upon the depositions from Louisa Wade, Fanny Weatherington and Dr Greenwood's observations on the health of the deceased child's body. It was also equally predictable that Mr Buszard drew attention to the difficult relationship between Mrs Wade and her daughter. Whilst he somewhat disingenuously claimed that he did not want to say anything harsh about the mother of Emma Wade and certainly did not wish to suggest that the behaviour of Mrs Wade contributed to the death of the child, he twice described the persistent requests to her daughter to go back into service as 'worrying and harrying her'.

The purchase of *Battle's Vermin Killer* was irrefutable, but the Counsel for the Defence insisted that it was bought by Emma Wade to kill herself, not the child. In a moment of magniloquence, Mr Buszard insisted that for the jury to believe that she had bought the poison with the intention of killing her own child would require 'a long leap in the dark before they arrived at that conclusion'.

The report published in the *Stamford Mercury*

only briefly mentioned the use of the letter written by Emma Wade to Henry Scarcliffe by the Counsel for the Defence and gave the impression that it had not received the attention which it deserved. The *Lincolnshire Chronicle*'s version of the address restored the importance of the letter to Mr Buszard's defence of Emma Wade, which he analysed in some detail.

In the view of the Counsel for the Defence, Emma Wade had only intended to take her own life: the statement in the letter which said that the child would be happy, did not refer to 'another world'. On the contrary, she knew it would be happy because the baby's father had done his duty and because she was leaving the child to the care of her sister, Mrs Weatherington and 'others who would be kind to it'.

Once more quoting from the letter, Mr Buszard, insisted upon a particular interpretation of the text. Emma Wade had written, 'So now, dear Harry, you must put me out of your mind'. The Counsel for the Defence pointed out to the jury that she had said 'me' and not 'the child'. Further, she had written in the letter that Henry Scarcliffe was absolved from any responsibility for the whole situation.

The defence of Emma Wade, at this point, was built upon the ambiguities of slippery words and may well have given the jury pause for thought. However, the reported continuation of the line of argument, which highlighted the virtues of Henry Scarcliffe, perhaps became more high risk when Mr Buszard claimed that his appearance in the witness box 'had been a terrible ordeal'. Unfortunately, he did not expand upon the nature of the ordeal, but merely insisted that Mr Scarcliffe 'had done all he could' and that Emma Wade was intending to leave her child to a 'loving father', asking him not to forget the child's name.

In one final emotive flourish, the Counsel for the Defence challenged the jury to answer the most solemn question: 'was that poor girl of nineteen, driven to such agony, to be sent by them to an ignominious death upon the scaffold?'

The report of the summing up of the case by the judge differed little from that found in the *Stamford Mercury*, with its sharp focus upon the letter written by the prisoner to the father of the child, as well as the requirement of the jury to be guided by the evidence rather than 'strong feelings of compassion'. The version of Justice Lush's reported words in the *Stamford Mercury* suggested a degree of scepticism about the Counsel for the Defence's interpretation of the letter. The *Lincolnshire Chronicle* similarly recorded those doubts, but also included a quite explicit dismissal of one of Mrs Buszard's key arguments in the defence of Emma Wade, based on the letter. He had argued that she intended to leave the child behind in the care of others: in the opinion of Robert Lush, 'there was not a word in the letter to show that'.

Whilst differing from the *Stamford Mercury* on the length of time the jury took to reach a decision, by twenty minutes, the *Lincolnshire Chronicle* did agree that throughout the trial, Emma Wade appeared to be in a stupor. On being required to stand, she needed assistance and in response to being asked by the Clerk of Arraigns if she had anything to say before sentencing, she said nothing.

Amid 'profound and painful silence in the court', Justice Lush passed sentence, hoping that Emma Wade would 'find pardon and peace'; she was then removed from the dock by the prison officials 'in the most kind and humane manner possible'.

The two extensive accounts of the trial had been published in Lincolnshire on Friday, 2nd May, but had been preceded by a number of newspaper reports published outside of the county, on Thursday 1st May. These varied in length and detail, ranging from a brief potted summary, found in the *Manchester Evening News*, the *Leeds Mercury* and *The Globe*, to the much fuller versions of the proceedings reported in the *Sheffield Independent*, the *Leicester Mercury* and the *Nottingham Evening Post*, although without reference to a possible reprieve, beyond the one implied by the jury's recommendation of mercy. Whilst these fuller versions gave a useful overview of the trial, they did not offer the kind of comprehensive particulars recorded by the *Stamford Mercury* and the *Lincolnshire Chronicle*.

However, a reading of the accounts does provide the occasional interesting detail not found in either of the two Lincolnshire newspapers. The *Nottingham Evening Post*, for example, recorded Dr Greenwood saying that he had treated Emma Wade with chloroform, as well as an emetic, on the evening of 18th April. More importantly, in the same newspaper, Louisa Wade said that as she had only been living at home for eight weeks before the poisoning took place , she 'could only speak accurately to the last two months'. The short length of time spent at home, perhaps adding to the domestic difficulties leading to the crime, was reported by other newspapers, but not the self-confessed limitation to her evidence.

The most interesting report in terms of extending the readers' knowledge and understanding of the trial is found in the *Nottingham Journal*, with its understated, matter of fact descriptions of Emma Wade's demeanour in court. The mundane details provided by the reporter, as well as the restrained account of her response to the sentence of death, suggest a high degree of first-hand reliability, compared to the predominantly melodramatic crowd pleasing descriptions found in several other newspapers.

During the trial, Emma Wade had been seated in

the centre of the dock, but whilst the jury retired to make its deliberations, she was re-seated to one corner, whilst another case was being heard. According to the *Nottingham Journal* reporter, on account of the repositioning of Emma Wade, the effect on her of the verdict was 'lost to the majority of the spectators'.

The effect was not lost on the reporter, however, whose description created the image of a woman who scarcely knew what was happening. On hearing the verdict from the Foreman of the Jury, she 'appeared stunned' and 'scarcely a sound escaped her lips'. The Clerk of Arraigns waited a few minutes before calling on Emma Wade to rise and receive her sentence. In her reduced state, she made 'several futile efforts' and had to be helped from her chair by a warder and a woman who had attended her in the dock and who gave her physical support, once she had risen from her seat. Eventually, she received the dread words of the law from Justice Lush 'in a half-fainting state'.

Finally, the prisoner had to be almost carried from the dock in 'an apparently insensible state', only becoming aware of the reality of the situation when reaching the steps which led to the prison below. At which point, 'her grief and fear found vent in loud and piteous sobs'.

The whole story of possible child murder in Stamford was tracked assiduously by the *Stamford Mercury*, for obvious reasons of local interest, but it only became an interesting news story for most other Lincolnshire newspapers once it had reached the Assizes. The *Sleaford Gazette*, 26th April, for example, only briefly reported the adjourned inquest in a column headed 'Miscellaneous' and was squeezed between the story of members of the royal family arriving in Paris and the safe arrival in New Zealand of seven hundred emigrants on the steamer Stad Haarlem.

The *Boston Guardian* had shown no interest at all in the story until it had reached the Assizes, publishing an account of proceedings on the same day as the *Stamford Mercury* and the *Lincolnshire Chronicle*. The impressionistic and occasionally fragmented report did a good deal to enhance the newspaper's growing reputation for inaccuracy, misinformation and the distortion of fact in the interest of sensation.

The censorious headline of 'Child Murder by a Policeman's Daughter', immediately orientated the reader's attention to an apparently shocking backstory. Just in case the reader do not pick up on the hefty hint, the information that the prisoner's father was a serving police officer was mentioned twice in the opening paragraphs.

Whilst the newspaper provided its readers with witness statements which established that Emma Wade had been unhappy before the death of the infant and that she had argued with her mother, it also included invented material to intensify the pathos of the young woman's plight, describing her lying on her bed during the day of the alleged murder 'evidently in great pain'.

Further sympathetic feelings in the reader were encouraged by the description of the 'feeble' prisoner having sat through the entire trial with bended head, 'having scarcely once altered her position' and who after hearing the sentence from the 'much affected' judge, was removed from court 'crying piteously'.

Any suggestion that the *Boston Guardian*'s account of the trial merely including material which the *Stamford Mercury* and the *Lincolnshire Chronicle* had chosen to omit is questionable in the light of Boston newspaper's version of the letter written by Emma Wade to Henry Scarcliffe, which was presented with a cavalier approach to both relevance and accuracy.

Inevitably, there are some minor textual variants, for example, 'return your portrait with heavy heart', found at the beginning of the letter, became 'return your portrait with a heart sadder than I can express'. However, other departures from the earlier published version, some of which were either quoted or referred to in the trial by the Counsel for the Defence, indicate that the later version found in the Boston newspaper was a misleading truncation of the text.

The version in the *Boston Guardian* completely

excises the final seven sentences in which Emma Wade declares her love for Henry Scarcliffe, as well as most of the many direct personal addresses of 'Harry', found earlier, effectively changing the whole tenor of the letter. The section of the letter excised included the statement absolving Henry Scarcliffe from any responsibility for the tragedy, which was utilised by Mr Buszard in his closing speech as a key piece of evidence.

Reprieve of Emma Wade from the Death Sentence, received by the Governor of Lincoln County Prison, 8th May, 1879

Emma Wade was condemned to death on 30th April: just over a week later, she received the news that her sentence had been commuted. The story of her sentence and subsequent merciful reprieve became subjects of extraordinary discussion and debate in the media, both in Lincolnshire and beyond.

The *Stamford Mercury* and the *Lincolnshire Chronicle* both published accounts of the process by which Emma Wade was reprieved; but each newspaper produced a very different report in terms of foregrounding who had played the most significant part in saving her from the hangman.

An apparently definitive account of the reprieve process was published in the *Stamford Mercury* 9th

May, and included copies of the letters sent from London to the Mayor of Stamford, informing him of the news.

According to the newspaper, the memorial sent from Stamford had been received by the Home Secretary, Richard Assheton Cross, who had immediately contacted Justice Robert Lush. That morning, Mr T G Mason, the Mayor of Stamford, had received a letter from John C Dalrymple Hay, the Conservative MP for the town, who advised him that the Home Secretary had commuted the death sentence and that the welcome news could be communicated to Emma Wade's friends.

To ensure maximum impact, the letter was published in full by the newspaper, alongside the enclosed official letter from Whitehall confirming the commutation of the death sentence.

108 St George's Square, 7th May, 1879

My dear Mr Mayor. The enclosed will inform you that the prayer of our petition has been attended to, and that poor Emma Wade's life has been spared. I saw the Home Secretary tonight, and he permitted me to say that this is an official communication.

I am yours very faithfully,
John C Dalrymple Hay

<u>Enclosure</u>

Whitehall, 7ᵗʰ May, 1879

Sir. Mr Secretary Cross having carefully considered the Memorial forwarded by you on behalf of Emma Wade, now under sentence of death, I have the satisfaction to acquaint you that he has felt justified in advising the commutation of the capital sentence in this case.

I am, Sir, your obedient servant,
A F O Liddell

On the following page, there was a paragraph headed 'The Condemned Convict at Lincoln', reporting a petition of two and a half thousand people, including county and city magistrates, aldermen, councillors, clerics and professional men, which had been signed and sent to Charles Seely the Lincoln MP, for immediate presentation to the Home Secretary.

The city of Lincoln had also clearly played its part in the reprieve of Emma Wade, but the newspaper report did not elaborate any further; instead it merely directed the attention of the reader to its previous page for further information relating to the outcome.

The *Stamford Mercury* seemed reluctant to let go of the Emma Wade story, as on a third page it printed a lengthy feature article from *The Times* with the title 'Crime in England', which reviewed the current state of criminality in the country in tones of despair and outrage. The scope of its analysis was a broad one, covering the domestic abuse of wives by their husbands, burglars attacking private property 'in imitation of the notorious Peace' and the alarming increase in the number of assaults on gamekeepers by poachers.

Towards the end of the article, the writer drew attention to 'one of the saddest stories which have come to light in the course of the present assize'. Emma Wade, a young girl of nineteen from Stamford, had been found guilty of murder and sentenced to death.

Unaware of her reprieve, the article recounted the facts of the case, speculating that she had been driven to suicide and infanticide by a 'fatal impulse of passion or of despair'. The narrative was generally sympathetic to Emma Wade, but the intention was more to do with using the case to illustrate a somewhat elusive point. The crime was 'as old as society itself, and resulting only too certainly from the conditions which society imposes'. In a particularly eloquent assertion, the writer suggested that, 'Such deeds as those of Emma Wade have been the staple of a thousand fictions and more than a thousand facts', concluding gloomily that, 'We can never hope to hear the last of them'.

As a response to an act of attempted suicide and infanticide, it was powerfully emotive writing, connecting both to the common fare of popular literature and the all too common newspaper reports on court business. However, as a serious analysis of the two issues, the article soon lost its way in a clumsy pile up of clauses and sub-clauses of pseudo-legal and moral distinctions, eventually crawling out from beneath the bombast with a welcome simple point: there is a world of difference morally, if not legally, between 'those who are betrayed into one crime, however heinous, and those who have chosen for themselves the career of habitual criminals'.

This section of the article concluded sententiously that 'the law must be stern to both, but the world, which is not called upon to pronounce judgement, will view the two differently'.

The relevance of the assertion to the reprieve of Emma Wade would not have been lost on the readership of the *Stamford Mercury*.

The report in the *Lincolnshire Chronicle* of 9th May, more or less duplicated by the *Sleaford Gazette* on the following day, highlighted the prominent role that Lincoln had played in the organisation of the petition.

Noting that the jury had made a strong recommendation for mercy on account of 'the cruel conduct which she had experienced at the hands of her mother' and that Mr Justice Lush had promised to forward that recommendation 'to the proper quarter at an early date', the newspaper celebrated the prompt and 'disinterested labours' of particular individuals connected with the city.

Mr John Giles of Guildhall Street in particular, had responded to the 'great amount of sympathy felt towards the poor girl in Lincoln' by 'directing this sympathy into a proper channel'. Mr Giles was instrumental in organising a petition requesting the Home Secretary to remit the death sentence and had been supported by MPs Charles Seely and Edward Chaplin. The petition amounted to two and a half thousand signatures and had been 'transmitted to London by early post'. Seely and Chaplin assured Mr Giles that they would place the memorial in front of the Home Secretary as soon as it arrived in London.

According to the report, several additional sheets which contained three hundred and fifty more signatures were also handed to Mr Giles, but were too late to be attached to the memorial.

Despite the headline of 'The Stamford Child Murder, Respite for Emma Wade' and an opening paragraph announcing that Major Edward Mackay, the Governor of Lincoln County Prison, had received a communication from the Home Secretary on the morning of Thursday, 8th May, the penultimate paragraph of the report gave the odd impression that at the time of publication, it was unaware that Emma Wade had been granted a reprieve. It expressed the hope that the efforts of Mr Giles and those citizens who had supported him 'will have the desired effect'. Yet in the final paragraph, the report informed the reader that the health of Emma Wade had improved considerably since having heard of her respite 'with feelings of intense satisfaction'.

The lack of any mention of Stamford in connection with the reprieve in the Lincoln newspaper and the marginalised reference to Lincoln in the Stamford newspaper creates a sense of competing claims for the prestige of successfully petitioning the Home Secretary. An attempt to reconcile the two divergent accounts of the reprieve of Emma Wade was undertaken by the *Peterborough and Huntingdonshire Standard*,10th May, which published the report from the *Lincolnshire Chronicle* overlayed with selected details from that in the *Stamford Mercury*. The result was a diplomatic hybrid in which a great amount of sympathy had been expressed for the poor girl 'both at Stamford and Lincoln' and Sir John Hay, Charles Seely and Edward Chaplin had jointly presented the memorials to the Home Secretary which contained 'no less than five thousand signatures'. Greater coherence was also established by switching tenses from 'will have the desired effect' to 'having the desired effect', although at one point the creator of the report, now dealing with two memorials, forgot his plural case agreements in the course of his worthy synthesis.

It was perhaps fortunate for the reporter of the *Peterborough and Huntingdonshire Standard* that he was unaware of a third party also craving recognition for having saved the life of Emma Wade.

Mr W J Douse was a man of strong opinions and a frequent writer of letters to newspapers on local and imperial matters. By his own admission, he penned glowing reports on his own public lectures on a variety of subjects, ranging from Game Law reform, the life of the Chartist James Sweet and Turkish atrocities in the Balkans. Not surprisingly, the self-advertisements of Mr Douse sometimes generated spikey conflicts in the press with disgruntled opponents who disagreed with his opinions nearly as much as they disliked his inflated sense of self-worth. A charlatan trading in mendacity and 'factious ebullitions' was one of the kinder evaluations of his public oratory at the time.

In a letter written to the editor of the *Nottingham Journal*, misdated 1st May and published 9th May, Mr Douse wished to draw attention to the subject of 'The Convict Wade'. At the close of one of his public lectures, he had alluded to the case of Emma Wade and his audience had subsequently pressed him to make public his letter to the Home Secretary petitioning a free pardon for her. He was submitting the letter for publication, as well as the reply from Richard Assheton Cross, although he also noted, in passing, that he had actually received two letters from the Home Secretary, one promising to investigate the case and a second, 'containing a favourable reply'.

The letter written by Mr Douse made it clear that he was, in his own estimation, a man of some consequence who got the job done:

> *Truman Street, Nottingham, May 4th, 1879.*
> *To the Right Hon. R A Cross, Secretary of State for the Home Department.*
>
> *Sir. I have been accustomed for some years to deliver lectures to my fellow citizens on Sunday evening, and this evening I drew special attention to the case tried last week at Lincoln Assizes, wherein a young person named Emma Wade was tried, found guilty, and sentenced to death by Mr Justice Lush, for the murder of her illegitimate child.*
>
> *The circumstances connected with the case are of a most painful nature, since it was proved that the poor girl loved, and kindly tended to her child; but, her mother, with whom she was living, kept up for six months a constant unpleasantness and worry, and eventually, the girl, in sheer despair, determined to end her life, and that of her babe also. By medical assistance the life of the mother was saved, but the babe died; and for this act she now lies under sentence of death.*
>
> *After explaining all the circumstances of the case the audience "nearly a thousand", many*

being respectable young women, carried with perfect unanimity the following resolution within the request that I forward it to yourself. "That the meeting heard with the painful feelings that Emma Wade was under sentence of death and most cordially supports the recommendation of the jury, when they gave the verdict, and we fervently commend the case to the merciful consideration of the Rt.Hon. Mr Cross hoping on an investigation he will advise a free pardon to her, who we feel, committed a rash act, when frenzy and despair rendered her unaccountable for her actions". Having thus fulfilled my duty, I am etc etc.

Whitehall, 7ᵗʰ May, 1879.
Sir. – Mr Secretary Cross having carefully considered your application on behalf of Emma Wade, I have the satisfaction to acquaint you that he has felt fully justified in respiting the capital sentence in this case. I am etc.

S (sic) F O Liddell

The numerous commentaries on the Wade Case, both in London and provincial newspapers, were sympathetic to the young woman, although it was evident that the outcome of both the trial and the petition for mercy were seen as useful material to support various contemporary ethical and legal arguments. It was certainly no coincidence that the second reading of the *Criminal Code Bill*, intended to either consolidate or improve existing criminal law, was being debated by parliament on 5th May, 1879.

A long article in the *Leeds Mercury*, 2nd May, was a level-headed and judicious analysis of the passing of the death sentence by Justice Lush, which argued for a reform in the law on murder.

The opening of the article presented a compassionate narrative of the circumstances which led to the death of an infant, drawing attention to the unreasonable pressures which had been exerted by Mrs Wade on her daughter and that Emma had 'taken affectionate care of the infant'. The writer of the article seemed to have a sound grasp of Mr Buszard's key defence that 'in the agony of body and mind caused by the taking of the poison herself' she had either given the child a small quantity or allowed the child to take it 'without any deliberate purpose whatever'. He also tentatively suggested, with some justification, that the Guilty verdict of the jury was ultimately influenced by the summing up of the judge.

On the whole, the description of the trial, was balanced and objective, although on two occasions it slipped into sensationalist opinion passed off as hard fact: Emma Wade had been 'led astray by her lover' and there had been an unquestionable causal relationship between the harsh language of the mother and her daughter's attempt to commit suicide 'in a frenzy of misery and despair'. The highly emotive word 'frenzy' does not appear in any other media account of the trial, but it was picked up, interestingly, by Mr W J Douse and his supporters in the motion presented to the Home Secretary.

Reprieve had not yet been granted, but the article was optimistic that the outcome was not in any doubt after the strong recommendation for mercy from the jury. More to the point, if her life was not spared by the Home Secretary, it would create 'a storm of indignation' which 'neither he nor any other Home Secretary would venture to face'.

Moving towards the central theme of the article, the writer suggested that if a particular sentence is allocated by the law to a crime of which a prisoner is found guilty, but it is not to be carried out, then that provided a strong argument for an alteration in the law. Specifically applied to the case of Emma Wade, if her execution 'would be universally felt to be nothing short of a judicial crime, the passing of sentence of death upon her is clearly an outrage upon public feeling'.

It was not the most tightly argued case for judicial change, the objective logic of the argument for reform being slightly blurred by the quasi-abolitionist rhetoric. However, the article confidently proceeded to support its argument by referring to the recent case of Henry William Pace, tried at the Central Criminal Court for the murder of Maurice Cole, his fellow workman and lodger, at Clerkenwell.

Henry William Pace had been found guilty of manslaughter and sentenced to eighteen months hard labour: he had been so affected by the mistreatment of his daughter by Cole, who had seduced her and then refused to marry her, that he had been close to suicide. The parallel with the emotional disturbance of Emma Wade, leading to alleged murder, was obvious, but the writer made the connection indisputably clear when he pointed out that the legal difference between murder and manslaughter was so indistinct that it was only by 'happy chance' that Pace was not convicted. By implication, the conviction of Emma Wade was the result of a converse unhappy chance.

On the basis of these two cases, as well as others in the past, what was urgently needed was a change in the law, 'which will draw a line outside homicides of a certain class and exclude them from the list of crimes punishable by death'.

It was a point of law, but is was also a point of public opinion: such reform was necessary to spare the English public from 'constantly recurring and most useless shocks to their sense of justice'.

Interestingly, the close association of the case of Emma Wade with that of Henry Pace, as part of the contemporary debate on judicial change, was also made by another Yorkshire newspaper, just over a week later. Reviewing the progress of the Criminal Code Bill through the House of Commons, the *York Herald*, 10th May, speculated that a member of the House was intending to move an amendment which, if carried would lead to the abolition of the death penalty. It further suggested that the recent cases of Emma Wade, Henry Pace and William Habron would be 'urged against the retention of the death penalty'. The newspaper did, however, concede, quite rightly, that such an amendment was likely to fail.

One of the more strange responses to the plight of Emma Wade was a letter published in the *Daily Telegraph and Courier*, 3rd May, which also found its way into the *Peterborough and Huntingdonshire Standard* and the *Wakefield Free Press* a week later. This letter, anonymously signed *Ion*, in its clichéd axioms and staid moralising, packaged the seriousness of Emma Wade's misfortunes into a grandiloquent, self-regarding sermon. The opening sentence immediately created the sense of being lectured: 'Justice is proverbially blind, and the law must take its course no matter how much the victim may appeal to our sympathies'. Mothers who murder their children and attempt to commit suicide, he insisted, are 'proper objects for the vindication of right'.

But the reader, of course, was being set up by the

writer, as he went on to qualify his seemingly absolute assertions with a guarded qualification. Maternal instincts are not usually murderous and when a woman kills her own child 'it is generally under the impulse of overwhelming grief or unreasoning despair'. This was the case of Emma Wade, a 'respectable domestic servant' who had given birth to a child after having 'yielded to love and temptation'. Her life with her parents had been so wretched that after writing 'a touching letter to her lover', she was determined to put herself and the child 'beyond the reach of further misery'. Anecdotally, the guilty mother was said to have been 'mentally depressed and unhappy since the birth of her child'; perhaps even more anecdotally, 'she was evidently of a weak and despondent nature'.

Having reached this point, *Ion* was ready to castigate the justice system and those who served it, with more than a hint of emotive abolitionist outrage. The twelve men of the jury did not have 'the faintest conception of the agony such a poor girl undergoes with no hope in the future and only unkindness and scorn for her present position'. Loftily, and with a clinching irony, *Ion* concluded with a triumphant aphorism: 'the tender mercies of the virtuous are often hard'.

That the writer was possibly a cleric is suggested by the direction which his exposition of the case next took. Such virtuous people as the jurors are unable to comprehend that 'looking wildly round for help and comfort, there is none in Heaven and earth until the pity of a Heavenly Father seems nearer and more bountiful than the justice of man'. Significantly, the only sentence which he quotes from 'the wretched girl's pathetic letter' is an overtly religious one: 'I hope the Lord will forgive me and take me to a home of rest'.

'Human love had failed her', he asserted, 'heavenly love seemed more kindly'.

Slipping dangerously close to vacuous sentimentality, *Ion* proclaimed that Emma Wade was 'no hardened atheist, full of murderous instincts like Charles Peace'; nor was she 'a danger to Church or State or respectable institutions': she was after all, 'only a poor tired servant girl longing for eternal sleep'.

Having defined Emma Wade in terms of having been a victim of uncaring justice, *Ion* proffered practical solutions for dealing effectively with such criminals as Emma Wade which were breath-taking in their crassness. What might have given her a chance of hope and reformation was either 'a sensible talking to by the chaplain' or 'a few kind motherly words from a good woman'.

The letter ended in smoking incensed pessimism, employing for effect an unacknowledged quotation from Samuel Johnson's poem, *The Vanity of Human*

Wishes, and declaring that unless Emma Wade had influential friends or the press took up her story 'to prove a moral or adorn a tale', she would be hanged and 'red-handed justice would be appeased'.

Whilst the trial and reprieve of Emma Wade presented an opportunity for the press to appropriate the story for its own polemical purposes, it was also an opportunity to engage readers on the level of pure sentiment and sensation, with little recourse to intellectual debate. The suspicious death of an illegitimate infant, a daughter driven to the edge of the abyss by a cruel mother, a romantic suicide letter, strychnine, a young woman condemned to death and hints of temporary insanity, all made for a compelling drama of human misfortune. The appeal of the letter written to the father of the illegitimate child, in particular, proved impossible to resist both as a strapline and an essential part of the narrative.

Soulby's Ulverston Advertiser and General Intelligence, 8th May, seemingly unaware of the reprieve of Emma Wade, or possibly choosing not to be aware of it, drew the reader into the report of the trial with the grim headline, 'Painful Case of Child Murder'. The alluring strapline beneath, 'A Pathetic Letter', recycled the same description found in the *Daily Telegraph and Courier*. With scant regard to the chronological framework of the case which had been heard in court, the report created the image of

Emma Wade as an affectionate parent, but who was 'mentally much depressed', a condition made worse by the repeated urging of her mother to leave home and go into service.

At the centre of the unfolding events was a letter written by Emma Wade which 'throws a light upon the prisoner's motive and her state of mind at the time of the fatal act'. For the information of the reader, the report printed the letter in full, noting that Mr Buszard's defence was based upon his interpretation of those parts of the letter referring to the baby, which had suggested that Emma Wade intended to commit suicide only, not kill her own daughter. In the interests of a kind of balance, the report also noted that the judge in his summary 'pointed out the probable meaning of the language about the child in the letter', but without sharing that probable meaning.

The version of the letter reproduced in the newspaper, and which had originally appeared in the *Pall Mall Gazette*, 1st May, contained an additional sentence to the text heard at the inquest in Stamford, which insisted that Henry Scarcliffe should remember Mrs Weatherington 'who had been a kind friend'.

On the same day, a hundred and thirty miles away, the *Sheffield Independent* printed extracts from the letter which also contained virtually the same additions to the text - the word 'good' being used rather than the word 'kind'. The context was not so much a report on the trial as a series of relaxed ruminations on the inconsistencies of the justice system, written under the heading 'Chit-Chat (By our Own Gossip)'.

Short on detail, but strong on emotive generalisations, the *Gossip* column expressed sympathy for Emma Wade, who had found herself in circumstances which it described as 'pitiable', and as a result she had been condemned to death. The letter, 'written on the eve of what she intended to be the last day for herself and her offspring', was described as 'one of the most touching eye ever read.' At which point, *Gossip* launched into a tirade on the subject of lenient sentences of twelve months imprisonment for parents who had deserted their 'little babes' and who had allowed them to 'starve to death through neglect.' If Emma Wade was to be punished more than such people, he concluded, 'it will be a blot upon the very front of justice.'

By far the most disapproving account of the broken workings of the justice system was published on the 10th May in *The Examiner*, a London publication which advertised itself as an independent weekly review of politics, literature, science and the arts. It was an astonishing piece of popular journalism, part rant, part social commentary, with an even more astonishing title of 'Emma Wade's Martyrdom'.

From the outset, the writer did not pull his punches,

claiming to be unable to explain what 'delusion' the jury was labouring under when it condemned Emma Wade to death. The only credible suggestion was that it had been 'bewildered' by the summing up of the judge, who had 'reminded the jury that their verdict must be based, not upon their feelings, but their judgement'. With undisguised contempt, after asserting that the judgement was 'cruel, rash and wrong', he suggested that the verdict had exhibited little feeling, but even less understanding.

The writer recounted the familiar story of the daughter of a police-constable forming an attachment to a jeweller's assistant which had led to the birth of an illegitimate child. The equally familiar narrative of a harsh mother was also revealed, but in language which left no doubts about the behaviour of Mrs Wade. The father of Emma Wade had treated her with patience and love, but her mother had 'subjected her to just that kind of persecution seasoned with taunt and insult which drives a feeble girl to despair'. What was clearly driving the malice in this version of Emma Wade's mother was a sense of shame connected to the embarrassing social circumstances of illegitimacy.

Included in the details of the events of Friday, 18th May, was a full version of the letter, as it formed 'a stronger appeal for mercy than any words of ours'. The version of the letter used by *The Examiner*, included the reference to Mrs Weatherington.

However, despite the assertion that the letter spoke for itself, the writer added his own analysis. In his opinion, 'a more beautiful letter was never written'. Its qualities of 'infinite simplicity and pathos' and 'gentle dignity and sorrow' made it a 'wonderful document for the pen of a domestic servant'. The reader was invited to 'note the tenderness of the thought' in the words, 'I have but one comfort, and that is I know my child will be happy', and place it alongside the last piteous words, 'I have sent you a piece of baby's hair'.

The letter was perhaps even more remarkable than the writer was aware: according to the entry in the *Lincoln Prison Nominal Record Book*, Emma Wade's level of reading and writing, like most of the prisoners, was described as 'imperfect'.

Switching its attention back to the court verdict, the writer claimed to be at a loss to explain how the jury with 'this document before them' and the 'poor heart-broken martyr herself facing them', were able to listen to their judgement, rather than their feelings, and return a verdict of Guilty.

To head off any objection that the writer was an apologist for infanticide, he robustly insisted that he had no sympathy for a mother 'however troubled and distressed who to save herself from ignominy or inconvenience destroys her helpless child'. It was a simplistic description of the social circumstances which might lead to the act of infanticide, but it served a purpose in that its bland general terms of reference contrasted with the distressing particulars relating to the case of Emma Wade. She was 'a poor, bewildered, distracted girl, herself almost a child'; having loved her child so passionately, she could not bear to hear it despised and spoken of with cruel scorn'; and so without any earthly hope, she cried out to God, 'Forgive me, take me - take both of us – to a home of rest'.

The silent embellishment of the letter written by Emma Wade might have alerted any sceptical reader to the possibility that the description of the events which had taken place in Stamford was perhaps nearer to the sensationalist fiction of a Wilkie Collins novel than the facts of a sombre criminal trial.

Predictably, the conclusion of this section of the article made an appeal to the reader's sense of pity 'too deep for tears', which 'every true-hearted man must feel'.

One of the complications of the case was that Emma Wade had attempted to kill herself and had therefore committed an additional criminal offence to that of child murder. It was a complication upon which the article expounded in a mixed mode of rational discourse and highly emotive hyperbole.

Its analysis began by lamenting what it saw as the inconsistency of a law which pronounced suicide to be a criminal offence whilst connecting every suicide with the exculpatory explanation of temporary insanity. By way of a contrast, the sentiment of public opinion pronounced that 'there are a thousand things so hard to bear, so terrible to understand...that suicide is sometimes the only escape from a great and seemingly endless difficulty'. This was especially true of those classes in society 'on whom the pinch of life comes sorest'.

At this point in the article, the reader might have been anticipating a sympathetic social commentary on the dreadful pressures of grinding poverty on the lower classes. Instead, the writer creates an imaginary scene of female suicide on Waterloo Bridge, by way of a pastiche of words taken from Thomas Hood's popular poem, *The Bridge of Sighs*. The subject matter of the poem, which was to later inspire work by Sir John Millais and G F Watts, was a gift in its pathetic description of a probably pregnant young woman having been driven to suicide by family rejection and public shame.

As well as adapting fragments from Hood's poem, however, the writer produced a new version of it in order to fabricate a connection with Emma Wade. In the original poem, the young woman throws herself into the Thames and drowns; in the version created by *The Examiner*, an imaginary 'broken-hearted mother' throws herself off the bridge clutching her child: she survives the suicide attempt, but the child dies. The sentimental rhetoric of pity and outrage continues with the contrived hypothetical question: 'if afterwards the mother were tried for murder and condemned to death, who would not feel his soul rise in passionate protest?'

Having evoked sufficient horror to create the necessary sense of shock, the writer goes on to robustly assert that there is little difference between the means of suicide being 'found in the Thames by moonlight or in the wretched packet of *Battle's Vermin Killer*'. Whether the story is told by a 'penny-a-liner newspaper paragraph' or 'by a great poet in an immortal song', the issues of motive and moral responsibility remained the same.

Had he read the article, it may well have come as a puzzling surprise to the entrepreneurial former mayor of Lincoln to discover that his mundane three penny packet of mouse killer had been linked with a famous poet's flights of fancy.

The process of reinvention by the writer continued with a doubling down on the horror and pathos of Emma Wade's attempted suicide and in the process seemed to abandon all restraint. The 'poor girl' wished to die, 'but loved her baby far too passionately to leave it behind'. In a tellingly imagined description, he deftly linked the events in Stamford with the poem by Hood, or more exactly with the writer's reinvention of the poem by Hood: 'in a moment of delirium' she clutched the child to her and '*sank*, as she believed, into slumber, confident in the mercy of God'.

Just in case the reader was still struggling to suspend all rational faculties, he or she was battered into submission by a remorseless barrage of mawkish religiosity, misleading fictions and quite ludicrous hyperbole.

'Picture her agony, her despair, when she drew back out of the very Shadow of Death', the reader was instructed, when Emma Wade awoke, not to God's mercy, but to the judgement of man. In a complete contradiction of the facts deposed in court, her infant lay dead on her breast, her heart broken and her brain 'still stagnified from its fatal sleep'.

The title of the article promised a narrative of brutality and death: the writer did not disappoint. In a paragraph which would not have been out of place in *Foxe's Book of Martyrs*, the judicial fate of Emma Wade was described in terms of pitiless cruelty.

According to the unfettered rhetoric, she was 'tortured back to life, dragged to prison, piteously tried', until the dreadful hour came when the judge assumed the black cap and sentenced her 'to be hanged by the neck till she was dead'.

It comes as something of a welcome respite when the writer assures his readers that the reprieve of Emma Wade was now secure and then proceeded to argue that the interests of justice would be best served by a 'comparatively short period of imprisonment'.

However, the champion of 'this poor martyred girl' was not finished. Like the *Leeds Mercury* and the *York Herald*, the writer drew a comparison with the verdict of manslaughter on Henry Pace; unlike the two Yorkshire newspapers, *The Examiner* stubbornly refused to discuss the comparison on a rational level. Henry Pace, an elderly working man, had only been given an eighteen month prison sentence for killing a man, whilst 'poor Emma Wade, a mere child of nineteen, for simply having tried to escape with her infant from the inhumanity of man' had been sentenced to death. In the opinion of the writer, a sentence half that of Henry Pace would be 'more than adequate to punish the girl Wade'.

In one final oratorical flourish, which seemed to combine a vision of the Fall of the Bastille with the spiritual challenges facing Christian in *The Pilgrim's Progress* as he fled the City of Destruction, the writer concluded emphatically: 'If there is any justice in the laws of England, if there is any pity in the hearts of Englishmen, if this is a Christian country, the prison gates will ere long be thrown open, and the poor would-be suicide, awakened from her 'temporary insanity', will pass forth to make one more trial of a wicked and a cruel world'.

Appendix One

Key Players in the Emma Wade Story

ALLENBY, H C. Served on Grand Jury at the trial of Emma Wade, at the Lincoln Assizes.

ANDERSON, Sir Charles Henry John. Served on Grand Jury at the trial of Emma Wade, at the Lincoln Assizes. Resident of Lea Hall, near Gainsborough.

ATTER, James Edward. Solicitor and Coroner. Presided over the adjourned and resumed inquest into death of Constance Mary Scarcliffe Wade at Stamford Town Hall. Resident of Stamford.

BARNETT, R W. Petitioned Home Secretary for

the reprieve of Emma Wade. Resident of Stoke Herrington.

BERGE-COUPLAND, Richard. Served on Grand Jury at trial of Emma Wade, at the Lincoln Assizes. Resident of Skellingthorpe Hall, Lincoln.

BRIGHT, John. Liberal MP for Birmingham. Petitioned Home Secretary for reprieve of Emma Wade.

BURTON, L. Served on Grand Jury at the trial of Emma Wade, at the Lincoln Assizes.

BUSZARD, Marston Clarke. Counsel for the Defence at the trial of Emma Wade at the Lincoln Assizes.

CROSS, Right Honourable Richard Assheton. Home Secretary. Reprieved Emma Wade.

DALRYMPLE, George. Police Sergeant. Gave evidence at inquest into death of Constance Mary Scarcliffe Wade, hearing at Stamford Magistrates' court and trial of Emma Wade at Lincoln Assizes. Resident of 4 Milner's Row, Stamford.

DALTON, Sophia. Petitioned Home Secretary for the reprieve of Emma Wade. Resident of The Grange, Morton, near Bourne.

DICKINSON, Frederick. Chemist and Druggist. Resident of 13 St Mary's Street, Stamford.

DOUSE, W J. Petitioned Home Secretary to reprieve Emma Wade. Resident of Nottingham.

EMERIS, William Robert. Served on Grand Jury at

the trial of Emma Wade, at the Lincoln Assizes. Resident of Westgate, Louth.

EVANS, Daniel John. Solicitor. Observed proceedings at the adjourned and resumed inquest into the death of Constance Mary Scarcliffe Wade. Represented Lucy Wade at the resumed hearing at the Magistrates' court. Resident of 40 High Street, St Martin's, Stamford.

FERREBY, John. Served on Grand Jury at the trial of Emma Wade, at the Lincoln Assizes. Resident of Wooton Hall.

FFYTCHE, JOHN LEWIS. Served on the Grand Jury at the trial of Emma Wade, at the Lincoln Assizes. Resident of Thorpe Hall, South Elkington, Lincolnshire.

GARFIT, Thomas. Banker. Served on Grand Jury at the trial of Emma Wade, at the Lincoln Assizes. Resident of Skirbeck, Boston.

GILES, John. Master Butcher. Organised memorial petition for the reprieve of Emma Wade. Resident of 17 Guildhall Street, Lincoln.

GREENWOOD, Dr Thomas Porter. Physician and Surgeon. Gave evidence at inquest into death of Constance Mary Scarcliffe Wade, hearing at Stamford Magistrates' court and trial of Emma Wade at Lincoln Assizes. Resident of 36 St Mary's Street, Stamford.

HAY, Sir John Charles Dalrymple. Conservative MP for Stamford. Petitioned Home Secretary for the reprieve of Emma Wade. Resident of 108 St George's Square, London.

HEGGATE, William Unwin. Former Conservative MP for Stamford. Alerted Sir John Dalrymple Hay to the case of Emma Wade.

LANGTON, Bennet Rothes. Served on Grand Jury at the trial of Emma Wade, at the Lincoln Assizes. Resident of Langton Hall, Langton-by-Spilsby.

LAW, William Farmery. Solicitor. Represented Lucy Wade, although absent from adjourned hearing at Stamford Magistrates' court on other business. Resident of 3 St Mary's Place, Stamford.

LEFFINGWILL, Dr Albert J. Petitioned Home Secretary for reprieve of Emma Wade. Resident of Brooklyn, New York.

LIDDELL, Honourable Adolphus Frederick Octavius, Under-Secretary of State for the Home Office. Informed Sir John Charles Dalrymple Hay MP for Stamford of the Home Secretary's decision to reprieve Emma Wade.

LOWE, Dr George May. Lincolnshire County Analyst. Gave evidence at the resumed inquest into death of Constance Mary Scarcliffe Wade, the hearing at the Stamford Magistrates court and at the trial of Emma Wade at Lincoln Assizes. Resident of 2 Cornhill, Lincoln.

MACKAY, Major Edward. Governor of Lincoln County prison, Greetwell Road. Received confirmation of the reprieve of Emma Wade from the Home Office.

MACONOCHIE, Alexander. Principal Clerk, Home Office. Coordinated reprieve documents relating to Emma Wade.

MASON, Thomas Gurney. Magistrate and Mayor of Stamford. Committed Emma Wade for trial on a capital charge in Lincoln at the resumed hearing at the Stamford Magistrates' court.

MASSINGBERD-MUNDY, Charles. Served on Grand jury at the trial of Emma Wade, at the Lincoln Assizes. Resident of Ormsby House.

MOORE, Colonel Charles Thomas John. Served on Grand Jury at the trial of Emma Wade, at the Lincoln Assizes. Resident of Frampton Hall.

NEVIL(E), Ralph Henry Christopher. Served on Grand Jury at the trial of Emma Wade, at the Lincoln Assizes. Resident of Walcott Hall, Stamford.

NEWMAN, Dr William. Surgeon. Assisted Dr Thomas Greenwood at post mortem on the body of Constance Mary Scarcliffe Wade. Resident of 7 Barn Hill, Stamford.

NORTON, Henry. Silversmith and jeweller, 73 High Street, Stamford.

PARKER, C J B. Served on Grand Jury at the trial of Emma Wade, at the Lincoln Assizes.

PARKER, William (Jr). Served on Grand Jury at the trial of Emma Wade, at the Lincoln Assizes.

REEVE, John. Served on Grand Jury at the trial of Emma Wade, at the Lincoln Assizes. Resident of Leadenham House.

SCARCLIFFE, Henry. Father of Constance Mary Scarcliffe Wade. Gave evidence at inquest into death of his daughter, hearing at the Stamford Magistrate's court and trial of Emma Wade at the Lincoln Assizes. Resident of 23 Broad Street, Stamford.

SIBTHORP, Charles. Served on the Grand Jury at the trial of Emma Wade, at the Lincoln Assizes.

SMITH, Etherington. Counsel for Prosecution at the trial of Emma Wade, at the Lincoln Assizes.

SMYTH, William Henry. Served on Grand Jury at the trial of Emma Wade, at the Lincoln Assizes. Resident of Thorpe Hall, South Elkington.

SWAN(N), William John. Apprentice to William Dickinson, chemist and druggist. Gave evidence at resumed inquest into the death of Constance Mary Scarcliffe Wade, hearing at the Stamford Magistrates' court and the trial of Emma Wade at Lincoln Assizes. Resident of Stamford.

TAYLOR, Major Robert John. Served on Grand Jury at the trial of Emma Wade, at the Lincoln Assizes. Resident of Burnham Manor, Barton on Humber.

THORALD, Charles. Served on the Grand Jury at the trial of Emma Wade, at the Lincoln Assizes. Resident of Heighington, near Lincoln.

THORALD, Sir John. Foreman of Grand Jury at the trial of Emma Wade, at the Lincoln Assizes. Resident of Syston Hall, near Grantham.

WADE, Ann. Mother of Emma Wade. Resident of 1 Palmer's Terrace, Stamford.

WADE, William. Police Constable. Father of Emma Wade. Questioned witnesses at inquest into the death of Constance Mary Scarcliffe Wade. Resident of 1 Palmer's Terrace, Stamford.

WALDO-SIBTHORP, Montague Richard. Served on Grand Jury at the trial of Emma Wade, at the Lincoln Assizes. Resident of Canwick Hall.

WARD, Richard. Police Superintendent. Charged with ensuring the safe custody of Emma Wade at the house of her father after the adjourned inquest into the death of Constance Mary Scarcliffe Wade. Applied to Stamford Town Council for financial support relating to the Wade case: refused. Resident of 30 Scotgate, Stamford.

WEATHERINGTON, Frances. Wife of Henry Weatherington, sawyer. Gave evidence at inquest into the death of Constance Mary Scarcliffe Wade, hearing at Stamford Magistrates' court and trial of Emma Wade at Lincoln Assizes. Resident of 16 Foundry Road, Stamford.

WRIGHT, Samuel Wright. Served on Grand Jury at the trial of Emma Wade, at the Lincoln Assizes.

Appendix Two

Summary Catalogue of the Contents of Home Office File 144/38/83390: Emma Wade

The descriptions below record the contents of the Home Office file relating to the reprieve of Emma Wade in 1879 and only made accessible to the public in 1980.

Editorial note: in the early stages of the process, the documents in the file passed through the hands of mainly anonymous Home Office clerks, who signalled their part in the process with a squiggled initial: these have been noted even though sometimes indecipherable. Some words have been abbreviated by the person dealing with the document when writing short Minutes, which I have expanded within brackets; words which were impossible to read I have signalled with a blank space within brackets.

Letter from Sir John Dalrymple Hay to Richard Assheton Cross, dated 2nd May, 1879

Home Office Notes and Annotations
- Stamped: 3rd May, 1879, Department 1
- Numbered: 83399
- Titled: Emma Wade, Spring Assize, Lincoln, 28th April 1879, Murder, Death, Mr Justice Lush.
- Docketed: Rt Hon. Vice Admiral Sir John C D Hay, Bt., MP, draws attention to this case thinks the poor girl was entirely out of her mind, asks that HS will consider the application which will come from his constituents (Stamford) and hopes that the sentence will be commuted
- Notes: Pressing; See within; Wait til petition comes, initialled Adolphus Liddell, dated 3.5.79; make official, written above text of letter, initialled; date of 2/5/79, initialled Alexander Maconochie

Letter from Justice Robert Lush, dated 4th May, 1879

Home Office Notes and Annotations
- Stamped: 5th May, 1879
- Numbered: 83399/2
- Titled: Emma Wade
- Docketed: Mr Justice Lush forwards Notes of Trial with observations and 'entirely concurs' in the Jury's "recommendation to mercy"
- Notes: Pressing; dated 5.5.79 [   ] with thanks, initialled; a clear case for commutation in my opinion, initialled JO; Letters of Reprieve [   ] to Judge; [   ] Sir John Hay and Dr Leffingwill; And ask Mr Justice Lush for what punishment he would recommend the Capital sentence to be commuted, preceded by a question mark, dated 6/5/79, initialled by Alexander Maconochie

Letter from Dr A J Leffingwill of Brooklyn, New York, dated 3rd May, 1879

Home Office Notes and Annotations
- Stamped 5th May, 1879, Department 1
- Numbered 83399/3
- Titled: Emma Wade
- Docketed: Dr A J Leffingwill states that he

has serious   doubts as to whether above was responsible for her act and prays for commutation of sentence. Offers to undertake the responsibility of conducting prisoner to America.

- Annotations: Pressing; initial with number 14; SO wrote 19.5.79

Letter from John Dalrymple Hay to William Unwin Heygate, dated 3rd May, 1879

Home Office Notes and Annotations
- Stamped: 5th May, 1879, Department 1
- Numbered: 83399
- Titled: none
- Docketed: none
- Notes: Initialled and dated 5/5/79; initialled next to word Official.

Memorial from the Rt. Hon. Sir John C D Hay, Bt. MP, undated

Home Office Notes and Annotations
- Stamped 5th May, 1879, Department 1
- Numbered: 83399/4
- Titled: Emma Wade
- Docketed: Admiral Rt. Hon. Sir J C D Hay, Bt., MP, forwards a copy of a Petition, now

being numerously signed by his constituents, praying for commutation of sentence of above.

- Notes: Pressing; Ack[nowledge]d Privately; see my Minute on 83399/2; date 6/5/79, initialled by Adolphus Liddell and Alexander Maconochie

Letter from Mr R W Barnett of Stoke Herrington, with newspaper cutting, dated 3rd May, 1879

Home Office Notes and Annotations

- Stamped 5th May 1879, Department 1
- Numbered 83399/5
- Titled: Emma Wade
- Docketed: Mr R W Barnett prays for commutation of sentence of above
- Annotations: Pressing; Ack[nowledge]d 6.5.79, initialled

Memorial petition signed by residents of Stamford, sent by the Right Honourable Sir John Dalrymple Hay MP

Home Office Notes and Annotations

- Stamped 6th May, 1979, Department 1
- Numbered: 833399/6
- Titled: Emma Wade
- Docketed: Admiral Rt. Hon. Sir John J C

D Hay Bt. MP, forwards Petition from the Inhabitants of the Borough of Stamford praying for commutation of the sentence of above, on the grounds stated therein.

- Annotations: Pressing; Act[ion] initialled twice, Ack[nowledge]d 6.5.79; John C Dalrymple Hay Bt. MP, Admiral, written on first page of Memorial, accompanied by Pressing and document number

Letter from Mr W J Douse of Nottingham, dated 5th May, 1879

Home Office Notes and Annotations
- Stamped 6th May, 1879, Department 1
- Numbered: 83399/7
- Titled: Emma Wade
- Docketed: Mr W J Douse forwards copy of a Resolution passed at a Meeting of the Inhabitants of Nottingham on Sunday the 4th inst. Praying for a free pardon for above on the ground that she committed the crime when unaccountable for her actions.
- Notes: Pressing; Ack[nowledge]d 6.5.79; Action with initial, initialled also by Alexander Maconochie; Informed of decision 7.5.79

Press cutting of anonymous letter submitted to the editor of the *Daily Telegraph and Courier*, published 5th May, relating to Emma Wade, sent by John Bright MP.

Home Office Notes and Annotations
- Stamped 7th May, 1879, Department 1
- Numbered: 83399/8
- Titled: Emma Wade
- Docketed: The Rt. Honourable John Bright MP forwards extract from *Daily Telegraph* drawing attention to the circumstances of the girl's crime having been committed under the impulse of overwhelming grief & unreasoning despair
- Notes: Pressing; Inf[orme]d of Respite 7.5.79; various underlining of words and sentences in press cutting with red ink; From Mr John Bright MP, Official, written next to pasted cutting, initialled

Telegraph letter from Edward Mackay, Governor of Lincoln Prison, dated 8th May, 1879

Home Office Notes and Annotations
Stamped: 8th May, 1879, Department 1
- Numbered: 83399/9
- Titled: Emma Wade
- Docketed: Telegram from Governor of

Lincoln Prison. 'The letter ordering the respite of Emma Wade under sentence of death received this morning'
• Notes: Pressing, initialled [   ]

Telegraph letter from Edward Mackay, Governor of Lincoln Prison, dated 9th May, 1879

Home Office Notes and Annotations
• Stamped: 9th May, 1879, Department 1
• Numbered: 83399/10
• Titled: Emma Wade
• Docketed: Telegram from Governor of Lincoln Prison. 'The letter ordering the respite of Emma Wade under sentence of death received this morning'
• Notes: Pressing, initialled [   ]

Memorial petition signed by citizens of Lincoln, dated 1st May, 1879 in title

Home Office Notes and Annotations
• Stamped: 9th May, 1879
• Numbered: 83399/11
• Titled: Emma Wade
• Docketed: Petition from the Inhabitants of the City of Lincoln praying for commutation of sentence of above & pleading that the crime

was committed by prisoner when in a state of mental derangement
- Annotations: Tell them decision, initialled by Alexander Maconochie; SO wrote 10.5.79

Letter from Mrs Sophia Dalton of Morton, dated 6th May, 1879

Home Office Notes and Annotations
- Stamped 9th May, 1879, Department 1
- Numbered: 83399/12
- Titled: Emma Wade
- Docketed: Mrs Sophia Dalton prays for commutation of sentence of above
- Notes: Tell her the decision, initialled by Alexander Maconchie, SO wrote 9.5.79

Letter from Edward Mackay, Governor of Lincoln Prison, dated 8th May, 1879

Home Office Notes and Annotations
- Stamped 10th May, 1879, Department 1
- Numbered 83399/15
- Titled: Emma Wade
- Docketed: Duplicate letter from the Governor of Lincoln Prison acknowledging receipt of respite
- Notes: initialled [   ]

Letter from Dr A J Leffingwill of Brooklyn, New York, dated 8th May, 1879

Home Office Notes and Annotations
Stamped: 10th May, 1879
- Numbered: 83399/14
- Docketed: none
- Notes: none

Letter from Justice Robert Lush, dated 15th May, 1879

Home Office Notes and Annotations
- Stamped: 15th May, 1879
- Numbered: 83399/16
- Titled: Emma Wade
- Docketed: Mr Justice Lush reports on this case. Thinks that the ends of justice would be answered by the infliction of one year's imprisonment with hard labour
- Notes and annotations: Pressing, ? Act accordingly, date of 16/5/79 initialled Richard Cross, Cond[itiona]l Pardon [   ] Judge

Appendix Three

Transcriptions of Key
Documents in the
Reprieve of Emma Wade

Document: 83399
Letter from Sir John Dalrymple Hay to Richard
Assheton Cross, dated 2nd May, 1879
(4 pages)

> *108 St George's Square, S.W.*
> *2nd May, 1879*

My dear Cross.

*A most piteous case of infanticide and attempted
suicide was first tried at Stamford and a poor girl*

named Emma Wade has been sentenced to death.

The whole story is a sad/one. Emma Wade is only 19, her parents are respectable, and her mother's strong sense of the disgrace of her daughter led to harsh and irritating conduct which however natural, led principally to the deplorable crime.

It seems to me that the/poor young girl was entirely out of her mind.

It is as sad a story as Effie Deans without a sister to plead for her life.

I write to ask you to consider the application which will come to you from my Constituents to (sic)/and to express my own hope that Her Majesty may be advised to remit the sentence of death by commutation to such a punishment as will satisfy the ends of Justice.

I am
Your very true
John C Dalrymple Hay

Document: 833399/2

Letter from Justice Robert Lush, dated 4th May, 1879 (4 pages)

Derby May 4th 1879

Sir

Emma Wade

I enclose my notes of the evidence given in the trial

of this young woman at Lincoln on the 30th April, for the murder of her infant child, a girl five months old. She was found guilty, but strongly recommended to mercy on account of the conduct of her mother.

The prisoner, who is only 19 years of age, had formed an attachment, to a young man, a shopman in / the same town, Stamford, and had her child by him. Her mother had become annoyed by her remaining so long at home and wished her to go back into service. The young woman took this to heart and determined to destroy herself and her child.

On the 18th April she bought a packet of "Battles Vermin Killer" and after writing a touching letter to the young man – which letter you will find set out in the evidence – she divided the poison into two portions, gave one to the child, & took the other herself. It happened that the portion given to the child contained the larger portion of the strychnine contained in the mixture / and nothing could be done to save the child. An emetic and the use of chloroform restored the young woman.

The case is one which evinces the deepest commiseration. The jury hesitated a considerable time but at length did their duty, adding the recommendation the record of which you will find at the end of the Notes.

I am informed that a Petition is in comte of

signature which you will probably receive in a few days.

The facts are clear and the law too but I would be glad if you could see your way to finding effect to the recommendation of the jury, in which I entirely concur. /

I go to Warwick on Wednesday and think probably be there til the beginning of the following week, after which I shall be in town.

I have the honour to be

Sir

Your obedient servant

  Robert Lush

Document: 83399/4

Letter from Sir John Dalrymple Hay to William Unwin Heygate, dated 3rd May, 1879

(2 pages)

108 St George's Square, S.W.
3rd May, 1879

Dear Mr Heygate
I am much obliged to you for your note as to the convict Emma Wade.

The Mayor of Stamford has sent me a copy of a petition now being numerously signed/ by my Constituents and he wishes me to shew it to Mr Cross. The petition itself will follow.

Perhaps you will kindly take an opportunity of letting Mr Cross see this Copy of the petition which is to follow.

Document: 83399/6
Memorial from the Rt. Hon. Sir John C D Hay, Bt. MP, undated

To Her Majesty's Principal Secretary of State for the Home Department

The memorial of the undersigned Inhabitants of the Borough of Stamford

Sheweth

1. *That Emma Wade, a domestic servant of the age of nineteen years, was on the 30th day of April 1879, at the Assizes held in Lincoln convicted of the murder of her illegitimate child and sentenced to death.*

2. *The said Emma Wade is the daughter of William Wade who for above 20 years has been, and is now, a member of Stamford Police force and who, during the whole of the said 20 years, has deservedly enjoyed the confidence of the Justices of the Peace and the Watch Committee for the Borough of Stamford and also the inhabitants of the Borough generally. On no single occasion has the said William Wade been found wanting in the discharge of his duties.*

3. The said Emma Wade was in the month of November last at her father's house delivered of a female illegitimate child and this child up to the day of its death on the 18th April 1879 was carefully nurtured and attended to by the mother who evinced great love for her child.

4. The said Emma Wade several times complained of ill treatment on the part of her mother, of her miserable condition, and of her inability to bear separation from her child, and in a letter of the said 18th April and addressed to the father of the child and read out in court, she made special mention of this alleged ill treatment and of her intention to kill herself. Your Memorialists would respectfully request your attention to this letter.

5. The said Emma Wade activated not by feelings of hatred or malice nor of pecuniary gain or other motives common in cases of murder, but retaining her love for her offspring took herself and also gave to her child on the said 18th April 1879 a quantity of Battle's Vermin Killer. The child died and the mother's life was only saved by careful medical treatment.

6. At the said trial of the said Emma Wade at Lincoln for the murder of the said child the Jury annexed to their verdict a strong recommendation to mercy - and in this

recommendation your Memorialists respectfully join.

7. *Your Memorialists respectfully invite your attention to the youth of the girl, to the misery she must have endured and to the absence of the motives common in cases of murder.*

Your Memorialists respectfully pray that you may be pleased to advise Her Gracious Majesty the Queen to commute the sentence of death passed upon the said girl Emma Wade for the murder of the infant child under the circumstances referred to.

And your Memorialists will ever pray etc.

Memorial petition signed by citizens of Lincoln - 1st May, 1879, appended
Document: 83399/11

To the Right Honourable the Secretary of State for the Home Department –

The memorial of us the undersigned residents in the city of Lincoln and the Immediate neighbourhood humbly Sheweth:

1. *That your Memorialists beg to direct your especial attention to the case of Emma Wade who was sentenced to death for the murder of her illegitimate child at Stamford at the recent Assizes held in the city of Lincoln.*

2. *That your Memorialists are of the opinion that all the circumstances attending the murder should be well-weighed and considered before the extreme penalty of the law is allowed to be carried into effect in this instance.*

3. *That your Memorialists are supported in this opinion by the evidence addressed at the trial for which they believe that the mother was truly fond of the baby and that she committed the act for which she has been condemned to be hanged while in a state of mental derangement.*

4. *That your Memorialists are further supported in this opinion by the strong recommendation of the Jury who tried the prisoner to mercy and by the remarks of the learned Judge in his summing up and the emotional feeling evinced towards the Prisoner by all who were in Court during the leaving.*

Your Memorialists therefore humbly pray that you may see fit to commute the sentence of death passed on the said Emma Wade.

And your Memorialists will ever pray etc.

Document: 83399/16
Letter from Justice Robert Lush, dated 15th May, 1879

(3 pages)

60 Avenue Road, May 15/79

Sir

Emma Wade

The further consideration which I have given to this case since the receipt of your form of the 7th instant with /No 83399/ in which you ask what punishment I would recommend to be substituted for the Capital sentence, induces me to regard it as the deserving of exceptional clemency.

Some of the essential elements of / Crime are lacking. The woman it is clear was not actuated by any bad motive, such as ill-will towards the child, or towards any other person or the desire to get rid of the child as a burden. On the contrary it was her love for the child which prompted her to take away its life. She had been goaded to the verge of despair by her mother who I have no doubt felt the disgrace brought on the family and rather than go out again to service, leaving the child in her mother's care, she made / up her mind to poison both herself and the child.

Under the circumstances I do not think that a severe punishment is called for, either by way of example, in the interests of society, or to deter the woman from a repetition of the offence, and I think that the ends of Justice will be answered by a year's imprisonment with hard labour.

I have the honour to be

Sir

Your obedient Servant

Robert Lush

Postscript

The Reprieve Examined

The media reports of the trial of Emma Wade were confident that she would be reprieved: the jury had strongly recommended mercy, there was a clear sense of local support in both Stamford and Lincoln for a reprieve and it was over twenty-five years since a woman had been hanged for infanticide. To some extent, there was also a perception that Justice Robert Lush, when placing the black cap on his head, was uncomfortable with the strict letter of the law being applied in the case.

The press, on account of its lack of access to most of the documents connected to such a closed process, made secure by the discretion of the politicians and civil servants handling it, inevitably remained on the outside of developments. The newspapers were able to offer bland reports relating to the prompt organisation of petitions by influential and well-placed figures as well as the final decision of the Home Secretary, but were unable to provide any further details. Even the open publication of letters by Sir John Dalrymple Hay in the *Stamford Mercury* added little to the interested reader's understanding of how and why Emma Wade had been spared.

An examination of the various documents in the Home Office file on the case provides some interesting fresh perspectives, which both extend and modify the reprieve narratives of the newspapers.

There was support for Emma Wade from different levels of society, some surprising, some less so; some from uneasy public figures with a public agenda, such as the Quaker MP John Bright, some from obscure individuals who wished to voice a private concern, such as Sophia Dalton, the former employer of Emma Wade.

The documents also reveal a range of different approaches to pleading the case for use of the Royal Prerogative.

Mr R W Barnett, in an early communication with the Home Secretary, chose to argue for mercy on a highly emotive level, reminiscent in tone and sometimes in its language of the article later published by *The Examiner*. The sentence passed on Emma Wade in his opinion was 'a frightful injustice': she was a young girl who had been driven mad by a 'heartless world and the nagging of her mother'. Having been determined to 'quit so wretched a life', she decided to take her child with her rather than leave it to 'the certain misery it would suffer after her own death'.

After enduring agonising pains, she had been 'dragged backed to life by a friendly hand in order that she may be hanged' (word underlined three times). In the opinion of Mr Barnett, Emma Wade had suffered enough both during the past fortnight and in the present, and should be restored to her home, asserting that 'the punishment already undergone is surely quite enough for a girl of nineteen'.

Having exhausted his emotive rhetoric, Mr Barnett paused to point out to the Home Secretary that such a course of action would meet popular approval: 'the heart of the People', he insisted, 'is powerfully touched by such cases and is always pleased by a large hearted exercise of the Godlike quality of Mercy to an unfortunate object'.

Mr Barnett's sincere concern for Emma Wade could not be doubted, although his rewriting of events in Stamford in the interest of saving her life could.

Perhaps the most bizarre letter to Richard Cross praying commutation was from a Dr Albert J Leffingwill, resident of Brooklyn, New York, but at the time located in Paris.

Dr Leffingwill had learnt of the case of Emma Wade after having read the article in the *Pall Mall Gazette* of 1st May, related to the trial. His understanding was that she had been 'abandoned' and had therefore attempted to commit suicide and at the same time kill her illegitimate child: having succeeded in the latter, she had been condemned to death.

He admitted that he had no knowledge of the circumstances other than what he had read in the newspaper report, but based upon the letter which Emma Wade had written 'previous to the commission of the act' and speaking as 'a medical man', he had serious doubts concerning 'whether at the time she was in her right mind or justly responsible for her actions'.

At this point in his letter, the medical man speculated that the Home Secretary would in due course be petitioned to commute the sentence to one of life imprisonment. He fully supported the granting of the Royal Prerogative, strongly suggesting that she be given a free pardon, but conditional upon her emigrating from the United Kingdom.

The strange suggestion became a quite extraordinary one when Dr Leffingwill volunteered to 'take the responsibility of seeing her to America where her story is unknown, and place under circumstances which shall enable her to obtain an honest livelihood and to return - it may be hoped, by a virtuous life, her past errors and to begin life anew'.

The convoluted syntax of the generous doctor's proposal was followed by the further suggestion that removing Emma Wade to America would be 'more beneficial than a lifelong imprisonment'. Admitting that he was working with only scant information, he asserted that he could not believe that that she was a criminal and was therefore capable of 'permanent reformation'.

The breezy optimism of Dr Leffingwill was followed by information concerning his movements between Paris and London during the course of the following weeks, and that he would be leaving for America on 28th May. Should the Home Secretary wish to communicate with him before 14th May whilst he was still in Paris, the helpful doctor provided the name of his London bankers, Messrs. Brown, Shipley & Co, Lothbury, as a point of contact.

Dr Leffingwill was informed by the Home Office in a letter dated 8th May that the death sentence had been commuted. The doctor, however, was not entirely satisfied to receive a letter without any kind of explanation concerning the ultimate fate intended for Emma Wade. On the same day, he wrote back to the Home Office to enquire whether the commutation decision meant life imprisonment or whether it remitted enough of her sentence 'to permit permanent expatriation – say to America – in lieu of permanent imprisonment here'.

The persistent doctor continued to press the Secretary of State with his idea of sending Emma Wade to America, hoping that it 'might be made feasible, and seem to you, not inappropriate or contradictory to the best interests – both of the State, and of the unfortunate individual concerned'. Perhaps sensing the need to justify his overweening persistence, Dr Leffingwill insisted that he had 'no sentimental sympathy with crime': his interest, he confessed, was based purely on his belief that the case was 'one for the Physician, and not for the Gaoler'.

Astonishingly, Dr Leffingwill continued his letter with the doggedness of an annoying door to door salesman. His idea was to take Emma Wade to America and have her placed, at first, as a domestic, in the family of a physician who happened to be a personal friend. The unnamed friend ran 'a large Hygienic Institution for the treatment – among other diseases – of various forms of mental derangement', which was situated in a small village on the outskirts of New York. Here, she would be 'under careful medical supervision, her suicidal tendencies watched and controlled, suitable employment furnished and opportunity offered for mental and physical improvement'.

The doctor reminded the Home Secretary that Emma Wade was still young and that if she recovered sufficiently and showed a desire to improve she would have other advantages by way of an education 'suited to fitting her for further usefulness'. In addition, she could also change her name and her past history would therefore remain a secret.

Like any good salesman, Dr Leffingwill offered the reassurance of personal testimonials should he be 'entrusted to oversee' the case: he was confident that the Home Secretary would deem his references to be 'satisfactory'.

Richard Assheton Cross, or whoever was reading the letter, might have thought that at this point the sales pitch was over, and that the doorstep philanthropist would have no more to say about his generous plan to rescue Emma Wade from herself. However, in one final throw of the dice, he regaled his reader with tiresome anecdotes of his ancestors coming over to America 'from one of the Eastern Counties of Old England' and who now populated every state of the Union. So far as he knew, he was the first person in his family to return to England for any length of time to enjoy 'her hospitable shores' and so he would be 'glad to help another of my English kin, to the possibilities of a New Life (underlined) in a New World', (also underlined).

At this point, the letter read like a discarded comic episode from *The Life and Adventures of Martin Chuzzlewit.*

It is quite probable that the eccentric letter from Dr Leffingwill did not make any contribution to the reprieve of Emma Wade. Similarly, but for different reasons, letters received at the Home Office on or after the 6th May, would not have played any part in the judicial reckoning, quite simply because a letter of reprieve was handed in to the General Post Office in St Martin's le Grand on the morning of 7th May for urgent delivery to the Governor of Lincoln prison.

The accounts of the reprieve process published in the *Stamford Mercury* and the *Lincolnshire Chronicle* emphasised the importance of the Lincolnshire petitions in support of Emma Wade as significant factors in the Home Secretary's decision making.

It is true that the petitions contained the names of many influential public figures, both in Stamford and in Lincoln. The Stamford document contained, for example, the signature of the Lord Mayor J G Mason, the Coroner James Edward Atter and ten Justices of the Peace, whilst the Lincoln petition was also endorsed by a number of Justices of the Peace, as well as by numerous clerics and worthy middle-class professionals working in the city. Surprisingly, there was no mention in any of the documents of the MPs Charles Seely and Edward Chaplin, who had reportedly put their weight behind the campaign to reprieve Emma Wade.

What appears to be somewhat inaccurate in the

press reports is the number of signatories to the petitions: the extant document for Stamford contains seventeen signatures, whilst that submitted by Lincoln has eighty-six. In both cases, the number falls well short of the two and a half thousand claimed by both newspapers for each petition. It may be that the Home Office had either lost or discarded numerous pieces of paper, but given the scrupulous record keeping at the time in relation to capital crimes and their remission, this would seem unlikely.

The impact of the petitions may have been minimised by their relatively late arrival at Whitehall. Whilst moves to formulate the memorials and to gather signatures were put into action the day after the trial, the time required to produce the documents, as well as ensuring their safe delivery to London, meant that they became less significant factors than implied by the media. The letter from Sir John Dalrymple Hay to Richard Cross stamped 3rd May, annotated with the instruction to wait for the petition to arrive, and his further letter, stamped 5th May, which gave assurance that a petition was 'now being numerously signed by his constituents', point to an unexpected delay in the process of gathering signatures: it was eventually received at Whitehall on 6th May. The Lincoln memorial and petition arrived at the Home Office even later: despite the document being dated 1st May, it was not seen until 9th May, by which time the decision to reprieve Emma Wade had already been made.

It seems clear that the key factors in the decision to reprieve Emma Wade were the personal intervention of Sir John Dalrymple Hay, writing to Richard Ashton Crosse on 2nd May, as well as speaking to him in private; and perhaps more decisively, the notes on the case penned by the trial judge, Justice Robert Lush, received at the Home Office on 5th May. The decision to reprieve Emma Wade was in all probability decided that day or at the very latest, the day after.

The subsequent judicial fate of Emma Wade, having been spared from the gallows, was decided by Justice Lush, whose opinion on the matter was requested by the Home Office. In the interests of justice, and in contrast to the post-reprieve sentence of Lucy Ann Buxton, he recommended that she serve a prison term of one year with hard labour only. The popular press, universal in its sympathy for Emma Wade, would have been appeased by the final outcome.

Ironically, in the 1881 Census, Emma Wade is recorded as being employed as the general domestic servant of Mr Henry Hawkins, a well-established hairdresser, and his wife Elizabeth, living on Church Street in Market Deeping, nine miles from Stamford. Rather than going through one of the various servant registries in the area, her position may well have been secured by way of personal connection - Mrs Hawkins, like William Wade, was born in the village of Wydonham in Leicestershire.

Perhaps in the interest of domestic harmony, Emma Wade never returned home after being discharged from prison on 27th April, 1880 .

Chapter Three

Selina Stanhope (1855-1932)

Selina Stanhope: Timeline

October-December, 1855: Selina Stanhope born in Langtoft, near Market Deeping, illegitimate daughter of Frances Stanhope.

22nd June, 1856: Selina Stanhope, baptised as Selina Deacon Stanhope, mother recorded as Frances Stanhope.

7th April, 1861: Selina Stanhope, age six, living with grandfather, Thomas Stanhope, drill man, age seventy-two, at Holbeach, along with Frederick Stanhope, his son, agricultural worker, aged thirty-eight and Frances Stanhope, daughter, housekeeper, aged thirty-three.

13th October, 1862: marriage of Thomas Dobney of Langtoft to Frances Stanhope.

18th October, 1863: baptism of Thomas, half-brother of Selina Stanhope, son of Thomas and Frances Dobney.

April-June, 1868: death of Frances Dobney.

2nd April, 1871: Selina Stanhope, wrongly recorded as Selina Standup, age fifteen, working as a general servant to agricultural labourer, John Hardy and his wife Mary Hardy, resident at Hurdletree Bank, Holbeach.

14th October, 1877: baptism of Thomas, son of Thomas and Elizabeth Dobney, stepbrother of Selina Stanhope.

1879: birth of William Edward Stanhope, illegitimate son of Selina Stanhope.

23rd June, 1879: Order of Admission to Bourne Union Workhouse for Selina Stanhope and her son, signed by the Relieving Officer, William Conington.

26th June, 1879: Selina Stanhope received into Bourne Union Workhouse, with her son.

17th July, 1879: Selina Stanhope and her son discharged from Bourne Union Workhouse, at her own request. They return to the house of Thomas and Elizabeth Dobney, her stepfather and stepmother, in Langtoft.

18th July, 1879, death of William Edward Stanhope by drowning.

23rd July, 1879: inquest into the death of William Edward Stanhope, in front of J G Calthorp, at the White Horse Inn, Market Deeping. Adjourned.

24th July, 1879: arrest of Selina Stanhope in Derby, on suspicion of child murder.

28th July, 1879: resumed inquest into the death of William Edward Stanhope. Selina Stanhope found guilty by coroner's jury of child murder.

29th July, 1879: committal of Selina Stanhope at Bourne magistrates court to Lincoln County prison to await trial at the Nottingham Assizes.

30th July, 1879: received into Lincoln County gaol, 9.30 am.

9th November, 1879: trial of Selina Stanhope at the Nottinghamshire and Lincolnshire Assizes, in front of Justice Robert Lush, for the wilful murder of William Edward Stanhope. Found guilty, but with a recommendation for mercy. Condemned to death.

25th November, 1879: reprieve of Selina Stanhope by the Home Secretary, Richard Assheton Cross. Sentenced to penal servitude for life.

3rd April, 1881: Selina Stanhope recorded in the Census as a prisoner in Woking prison, Surrey, a former domestic servant and unmarried.

24th May, 1889: Licence granted by Henry Matthews, Home Secretary, discharging Selina

Stanhope from Woking prison, conditional upon being confined at the Elizabeth Fry Refuge in Hackney 'so long as such Licence remain in force'.

19th October, 1889: Conditional Licence exchanged for an Ordinary Licence.

6TH November, 1889: released from Elizabeth Fry Refuge to live at the house of Mrs Vinter, 38 Great Percy Street, Pentonville, without police supervision.

5th April, 1891: recorded as an unmarried domestic servant, resident at 38 Great Percy Street, Pentonville, house of William Vinter, aged thirty-nine, maker of ivory plaques, mathematical dividers and engraver; Mary Vinter, aged thirty-five (wife); Ethel Vintner, (daughter), scholar; Eliza Cooper, mother-in-law, aged sixty-nine, parish of St Phillip's, Clerkenwell, London.

1897: marriage of Selina Stanhope to Thomas Murshed Lamb in West Ham.

1911: resident at Blackbird Street, Potton, Bedfordshire, with husband Thomas Murshed Lamb, licensed victualler, aged fifty.

1931: death of Thomas Murshed Lamb.

April-June, 1932: death of Selina Lamb (née Stanhope) in West Ham, aged seventy-seven years.

Mud and Stuff: The condemnation and reprieve of Selina Stanhope

<u>1879...</u>

....impoverished, deprived and neglected, pushed to the edge by the familiar disasters of bad harvests brought on by the wet seasons, Langtoft bravely existed and endured.

The village might have been partially rescued from sombre anonymity by the seductive sibilance and assonance of mid-Victorian pastoral poetry or from elusive obscurity by solid facts, uncovered by earnest antiquaries digging around Crowland Abbey with their slippery speculations, or dredging through unplumbed documents for evidence of the disappeared: but it wasn't.

<u>1879...</u>

....rooted, fixed and reduced, defined by the strict expectations of religious observance, by the even stricter obligations of manorial courts and the unarguable demands of an empty stomach, impoverished villagers of Langtoft acquiesced and accepted the grim reality that both the present and the future were merely the past, dressed up in not very fancy clothing.

The village may have been temporarily saved from an overwhelming sense of grinding sameness by the annual treat for teachers and children attending the Church Sunday School, set up on the vicarage lawn, or by a week of special religious services organised by the Congregational Chapel, involving sermons and addresses which were 'plain, earnest and practical'. But there was a limit to the liberating power of a one-off meat tea, cricket in the paddock and a humorous lecture delivered by Mr Parker of Peterborough on 'Classes who Suffer'.

The irony of Karl Marx having visited Langtoft a few years earlier to observe and record the wretched living conditions which he had found in twelve of its houses and who had delivered his own less than humorous lecture on the subject of classes who suffer, seemed not to have been noticed by Mr Parker.

1879...

....in the village on the edge of the Fens, on Tuesday, 22nd July, the same became shockingly different, as death by water took an inexplicable turn when the body of a drowned boy, seven months old, was fished out the muddy waters of a drain and the reclamation of the truth of the matter from the murky depths of the life of Selina Stanhope began.

Inquest into the Death of William Stanhope, before J G Calthorp, at the White Horse Inn, Market Deeping, Wednesday 23rd July, 1879

The restrained headline of 'Supposed Infanticide' which prefaced the report on the inquest into the unexplained death of seven month old William Stanhope, published in the *Stamford Mercury* of 25th July, 1879, was in contrast to the report itself. The disturbing account of the inquest's findings made it clear that the death of a small boy found face down in a drain was not thought to be accidental and that the mother of the child, Selina Stanhope, aged twenty-three, was the prime suspect in the killing of her son.

According to the newspaper, the naked body of the child had been discovered by William Holmes, a Langtoft farmer, on the previous Monday. Specifically, it had been found in a drain by the side of the turnpike road between Langtoft and Market Deeping. A post mortem examination by William Deacon, surgeon of Market Deeping, revealed that the child had died from drowning and had been in the water for a several days.

The body had been identified as the illegitimate son of Selina Stanhope, who had been last seen with the child on Friday 18th July, sitting near the bridge over the drain which crossed the turnpike road.

Suspicion of foul play was suggested by the young woman having returned home that night without the child and her having disappeared from the village on the following day.

The inquest was adjourned until Monday, 28th July, in order to allow Thomas Pawson, the Inspector of Police at Bourne, who had fished the child out of the water, the time to track down the suspect.

The headline 'Strange Affair at Langtoft' used by the *Grantham Journal*, published the day after the *Stamford Mercury* and available every Saturday in the village from the local agent, Mr Peasgood, was less circumspect and deliberately calculated to intrigue. The focus, not surprisingly, was upon the details of the supposed crime rather than on the inquest proceedings, and suggested that their reporter had been digging around the village and had unearthed additional material, some of it unsavoury.

The opening of the report highlighted a 'very startling discovery' which had been made on the previous Tuesday morning, rather than on the Monday morning reported by the *Stamford Mercury*: Mr Holmes, a Langtoft farmer, was driving his cart from the village to Market Deeping and after stopping to clean his boots had been 'startled to see the dead child in the water'. Mr Holmes drove on to Market Deeping and reported the matter to Inspector Pawson, and both returned to the spot, where the police officer lifted the dead child out of the drain. The body was then taken to Mr Deacon's surgery, where the doctor examined it, before depositing it at the White Horse Inn, Market Deeping, in anticipation of an inquest.

The potential crime having been described, the story then focused upon the police investigation and the pursuit of a suspect. Inspector Pawson began his enquiries in the village of Langtoft and 'had little difficulty' in identifying the dead body, although the newspaper did not reveal how this rapid result was achieved. Whatever methods he had used, the inspector established that the deceased was the 'illegitimate female child of Selina Stanhope, aged eight months'.

The child's mother was certainly Selina Stanhope and it was equally certain that it was illegitimate; what either the inspector or the newspaper got wrong was both the gender and the age of the mystery infant found dumped in a drain.

After further enquiries by Inspector Pawson, it emerged that Selina Stanhope had left her father's house on the previous Friday, at about 6 o'clock in the evening, taking her child with her, and intending to go to Market Deeping. She had returned to the house, three hours later, but without the child, and claimed that she had 'put it out to nurse' in the Towngate area of Market Deeping.

The following morning she left the house, taking her boxes and wearing apparel with her, but had refused to say where she was going.

Acting upon further information, Inspector Pawson was despatched to Derby, where Selina Stanhope was arrested on the Wednesday morning and brought back to Bourne. If the chronology of the newspaper account was accurate, the efficiency of the police investigation had been impressive.

Having established the background to the case, the *Grantham Journal* confirmed that an inquest had been held on the death of William Stanhope which involved the identification of the body by several witnesses. A post mortem examination had been carried out by Mr Deacon, who said that he had not found any marks on the body, but was of the opinion that the child had been put into the water alive and had subsequently suffocated.

The reader was informed that the inquest had been adjourned until 6 o'clock on the following Monday, adding that Selina Stanhope had been brought before a special meeting of the magistrates on the day after the adjourned inquest and remanded in custody until Tuesday, 29th July.

The follow up report by the *Stamford Mercury* published on 1st August, with the significantly adjusted headline of 'Infanticide', provided its readers with a great deal more information from the adjourned inquest which had been only briefly reported the week before.

Several of the witnesses appearing at the coroner's court were clearly there to identify the body of the dead infant, but they also provided useful information concerning the depressingly miserable life of Selina Stanhope.

Edgar Jenner, Master of the Bourne Union Workhouse, confirmed that the body was that of the child of Selina Stanhope, a single woman, who had been admitted as a destitute pauper on 20th June, 1879, by order of the Relieving Officer, William Conington. She had remained there with her child for about three weeks, but left on Thursday, 17th July, having handed in her discharge papers the day before: she had not given a reason for leaving. It may be an example of misreporting, rather than the Master's mistake, but the *Bourne Union Workhouse Register of Admissions and Discharges*, written in Edwin Jenner's own hand, records that Selina Stanhope and her child were admitted by William Conington on 23rd June and were received into the workhouse on the morning of 26th June.

Elizabeth Dobney, wife of Thomas Dobney, of Langtoft, also confirmed the identity of the body as being William Stanhope, but her additional information was more anecdotal than that of Edgar Jenner and in some respects seemed to be quite hostile. Mrs Dobney confirmed that she knew Selina Stanhope and the child, but what she didn't appear to mention, and it certainly was not reported, was that she was her stepmother and had played a significant part in the dismal domestic drama.

She deposed that Selina Stanhope and the child had stayed at her house until 6 o'clock on the night of Friday, 18th July, at which point she left to seek lodgings after having been told by the witness that she 'could not keep her any longer'. No explanation for this ultimatum was offered to the court by Mrs Dobney, but an examination of the Census records suggests the economic and spatial difficulties of a family of four children, aged between four and fifteen, and an elderly husband of sixty-two years of age, who may well have been unfit to work at the time: Thomas Dobney was buried just over six weeks later, on 11th September, 1879.

Selina Stanhope had returned to the house between 9 and 10 o'clock that night, but without her baby. On enquiring about the child, Mrs Dobney was told that she had taken it to Towngate in Market Deeping, where it would be taken care of by a nurse. She had then packed her box and told Mrs Dobney that she was going to the house of John Reedman, a local coal merchant.

Up to this point, the evidence of Mrs Dobney was arguably a measured presentation of difficult domestic circumstances. However, the final part of her deposition seems to have become more strident, suggesting a degree of tension and dislike between the two women.

Mrs Dobney made it clear that Selina Stanhope had stayed the night at her house, despite not being welcome, and made it doubly clear that 'she never seemed to care much about the child' and that 'she was always saucy to me when spoke to'.

The more restrained deposition of Mr Deacon, in its his professional objectivity, went some way towards dispelling the air of domestic toxicity in the courtroom. After the jury had viewed the body of the unfortunate William Stanhope, he had performed the post mortem which confirmed that the little boy had suffered no physical violence, but based upon the content of the stomach and the condition of his lungs, he had almost certainly died in the water from drowning.

The deposition of William Holmes, who had discovered the body, was largely a duplication of that reported in the *Grantham Journal*, although it contained the useful additional information that the spot where he had discovered the body was only about half a mile from where Mrs Dobney lived. He also described in rather graphic detail his discovery of the corpse of William Stanhope: the child was lying on his face, his head in the water, which covered the child entirely apart, perhaps, from his feet.

At this point, the report moved on to record important witness depositions which had not been mentioned in any of the two early accounts of the inquest. All three were eye-witness accounts from local land workers who had seen Selina Stanhope by the bridge at around 7.30 on the evening of Friday, 18th July, in a state of some distress.

James Jackson had been on his way home to Langtoft, having stayed late in Market Deeping to do some additional haymaking because of the fine weather that day, along with Joseph Cook and Henry Bell. On seeing her, he stopped his cart and asked how she was, but did not receive a reply. Mr Jackson then kindly offered Selina Stanhope a lift home, but she declined the offer, saying that she was on her way to Market Deeping, which was in the opposite direction.

Perhaps sensing that something was not quite right, he had said, 'Don't hurt the babe', and the other two men apparently expressed pity for her. James Jackson said that he did not know why he had said those words, but confirmed that he had seen the child in a basket close by its mother and it was dressed in a shawl or a dark jacket. Mr Cook had said somewhat obscurely at the time that it was 'a bad job she had happened of it', perhaps referring to her having had an illegitimate child.

The three men then left her at the bridge, but

not before James Jackson repeated his uneasy words about not hurting the baby, adding 'it will earn you a bit of bread when you can't get it.' There was again no response from Selina Stanhope, but Mr Jackson did not press his concern for the safety of the baby any further, 'fearing I might get into trouble': unfortunately, he did not elaborate upon what he meant by this.

Thomas Holmes was then recalled to confirm the exact location of the drain where he had found the child, stating that it was the one near the field owned by Thomas Cave; James Jackson was also recalled, corroborating the deposition of Thomas Holmes when he told the court that he had spoken with Selina Stanhope by the bridge 'nearest Deeps, and about two or three hundred yards from the one near Mr Cave's field'.

If Selina Stanhope had been treated somewhat uncharitably in her hour of need by her stepmother, the reception she received from Sarah Fowler, wife of Chelsea Pensioner, Francis Fowler, when she knocked on her door, was quite the opposite.

She had arrived at Mrs Fowler's house sometime between 8 and 9 o'clock on the Friday evening and was clearly in some discomfort: she had fallen against the door and had to support herself with her hand. Mrs Fowler was concerned about the young woman and invited her into the house. An exchange of pleasantries moved on to Selina Stanhope explaining to Mrs Fowler that she intended to leave Langtoft the next day and that she had been trying to borrow a barrow in which to transport her box. She also told Mrs Fowler that she had 'put her child out' to a nurse.

The young woman went away, but returned at some point between 9 and 10 o'clock to ask for a drink of water. The kindly Mrs Fowler insisted that she came in to have a cup of tea and a piece of bread and butter. She did so, but in her distressed and weak state, she was unable to eat. The conversation once more turned to William Stanhope and his whereabouts, the mother reassuring Mrs Fowler that he was in good hands and would be well cared for. Further, when she got to Derby, she intended to send the child some money, as there was work to be had there, unlike in Langtoft. If the words of Mrs Fowler were correctly reported, Selina Stanhope had said somewhat disparagingly that she was happy to leave the village and never set foot in it again. Before leaving, she added that she thought it unlikely that she would get back into her step-parent's house, as they had told her to go away to where she had left her child. Mrs Fowler reassuringly suggested that she would be able access the house as she had her little brother with her.

Resumed inquest into the Death of William Stanhope, before J G Calthorp, at the White Horse Inn, Market Deeping, Wednesday 23rd July, 1879

The report in the *Stamford Mercury*, continued its comprehensive coverage of the case with details of the further developments at the resumed inquest. The initial inquest had been adjourned until Police Inspector Pawson had completed his enquiries and it was therefore no surprise that his deposition was deemed critical.

He reminded the court that he had removed the body from the drain and had taken it to the White Horse Inn. He added that he had conducted a careful examination of the area for footmarks where the body had been discovered and had found that the grass had been trodden down where someone had slipped into the water.

More decisively, on 23rd July, he had tracked down Selina Stanhope at 25 Bridge Gate, in Derby, over sixty miles away from Langtoft: it was either an astonishing piece of detective work or Inspector Pawson had been tipped off by a reliable informant in the village, possibly Mrs Fowler.

The deposition of the Inspector in its staid meticulousness, structured around the routine enquiry formula of 'I said/she said', created the impression of reading verbatim from his notebook. The inspector had asked her if she came from Lincolnshire: she had replied in the affirmative. He then asked her if she was the mother of an illegitimate male child: she once again replied in the affirmative. At this point, the full weight of official procedure swung into action against Selina Stanhope in all its formulaic gravitas: 'I am a police officer from Lincolnshire and about to arrest you, and I caution you on what you say as it may be taken down in writing, and given in evidence against you. I shall apprehend you on the charge of wilfully murdering your child at Langtoft on Friday 18th of this month by drowning it in a ditch by the roadside near the bridge known as Nidd's Bridge': this time, Selina Stanhope made no reply.

If reported correctly by the newspaper, it was a curiously clumsy and defective declaration by the inspector, in that he could not properly arrest Selina Stanhope for the murder of her child, only on suspicion of having murdered her child. If the faux pas was true, it might have put the coroner's jury in a difficult position when arriving at a verdict: it could hardly judge Selina Stanhope to be Not Guilty when she had already been arrested and formally charged by the police.

However, in the final part of his deposition, the inspector resolved any such awkward conflict in the procedure by providing additional information, less formally presented to the court than reading from an official notebook.

He had found some child's clothes and the accused woman had told him that she was going to send them to the people who were looking after her child in Market Deeping. More damning, whilst conveying Selina Stanhope to Bourne police station, 'she was fretting' and asked if her child had been found? The taciturn inspector simply replied in the affirmative, to which she allegedly responded, 'I wish I was with it: I wish I had not done it. I know I shall have to be punished for it'.

After hearing other evidence which corroborated earlier depositions and the lucid summing up of the main points by the coroner, a no doubt relieved jury had taken only a few minutes to reach a verdict of wilful murder.

The prisoner was taken to appear before the Bourne magistrates the following day and committed for trial at the next Assizes.

One of the many problems facing the modern reader of contemporary newspaper reports of nineteenth-century criminal trials is not the lack of information, but quite often the excess of it. Accounts of inquests, trials and executions when reported by different newspapers, even within the same geographical region, often construct narratives which complement each other, but occasionally produce puzzling contradictions, especially in terms of who said what.

To some extent, such difficulties arise from reporters, or their editors, choosing to excise particular details in the interest of space or because a judgement call was made on what was essential to the creation of a seemingly authentic story.

The decision to include some details and not others, in the final analysis, may make little difference to the reader's understanding of the totality of the narrative, but occasionally such omissions or inclusions create a sense of two and sometimes more conflicting versions of the same trial for the reader to consider.

The account of the inquest, published on 2nd August in the *Grantham Journal*, with the headline 'Distressing Case of Infanticide at Langtoft', unlike the *Stamford Mercury*, published the day before, helpfully provided the reader with a full list of jurors, who were drawn mainly from tradesmen and farmers living in and around Market Deeping:

James Holland (Foreman)
James Buzzard
Samuel Charity
Thomas Chesterfield
Joseph Churchman
Elijah Dixon

William Harrison

R Longfoot

Thomas Nurse

Joseph Sanderson

William Shillater

Frederick Swift

The report of the various depositions, on the whole, replicate those found in the *Stamford Mercury*. Occasionally, however, a witness was reported as having included small details in their depositions not mentioned in the earlier newspaper - such as Sarah Fowler having quizzed Selina Stanhope as to whether she had left her child in Langtoft or in nearby Baston, but having tactfully backed off the subject when she did not get a definitive response. Similarly, William Holmes, the farmer who had discovered the body of the child, gave the information to the court that the grass by the drain side had been trodden down, but there was no sign of a struggle having taken place.

The reported words spoken by Mrs Fowler reinforce the sense of her concern for the safety of William Stanhope and for the wellbeing of his mother, and the observations of Mr Holmes suggest that he had possibly been in conversation with Inspector Pawson at the side of the drain after the body had been removed, but neither make any significant impact on an understanding of the case.

The report of the inquest in the *Stamford Mercury* had briefly touched upon clothes belonging to William Stanhope having been found in the possession of his mother when arrested at Derby by Inspector Pawson. However, the *Grantham Journal* seemed to attribute a greater significance to the discovery by noting that both Edgar Jenner and Eliza Dobney had made detailed reference to the clothes in court and that both were pressed by the coroner for further information: Mrs Dobney had seemed especially pleased to oblige.

Edwin Jenner had been able to describe some of the clothes which William Stanhope was wearing when the mother left the workhouse: blue shoes, a plaid shawl and a light-coloured flannel hood. Elizabeth Dobney was able to supply more detailed information about the clothes which she had observed when Selina Stanhope departed the house. The boy was wearing a magenta coloured dress, a blue and white hood, blue shoes, a red and white checked shawl, a little worsted fall and a white pinafore. Mrs Dobney had enthusiastically assured the court that, 'I should know them all if I could get a sight of them'.

She was given the opportunity to view the clothes in court and confirmed that they were indeed the same clothes which she had described earlier. Mrs Dobney gave added value to her evidence by revealing that she had noticed a fold in the waistband of one of the flannel petticoats and there was such a fold in the petticoat worn by the child. By way of further assurance, she told the court that she had seen the mother put the child into the petticoat and had noticed the fold at the time.

In sharp contrast, Edgar Jenner, who it seems was not such a skilled observer of incriminating folds in infant clothes as Mrs Dobney, simply confirmed that the plaid shawl which had been shown to him in court was the one worn by William Stanhope, but without any further elaboration.

The reporting of the deposition of Inspector Pawson by the *Grantham Journal*, which was central to the business of the adjourned inquest, duplicated a good deal of the material published in the *Stamford Mercury* the day before, but created a less officious image of the policeman. In line with its focus on the clothing of William Stanhope, it also reported additional material concerning the arrest of Selina Stanhope in Derby.

On apprehending the young woman, the inspector had asked her whether or not she was from Lincolnshire. He then informed her that her child had been found drowned and it had been conclusively identified as belonging to her. In the questionable version published in the *Stamford Mercury*, Selina Stanhope had been promptly charged with murder and reminded of her right to remain silent. In the *Grantham Journal*'s version, there is no mention of this procedure having taken place. Rather, the inspector demanded to see what she had in her unlocked box, to which she made no objection. The inspector then listed for the benefit of the court the clothes which he had found and had brought with him to the inquest: a red and black checked shawl, a magenta braided frock, a swathe, two flannel petticoats, one pinafore, a fall and a pair of shoes. In addition, Inspector Pawson had brought along a blue and white hood, which had been handed to him by Detective Clark of the Derby police, who had recovered it from a vault at 25 Bridge Gate.

The various items of clothing found in the box were held up for the benefit of the court and were confirmed as those belonging to William Stanhope by both Edgar Jenner and the eagle-eyed Elizabeth Dobney.

Whilst he had been tying the clothes up, Selina Stanhope had told the inspector that she was intending to send the clothes to the people in Market Deeping who were taking care of her child. Her confession of guilt on the way to Bourne, recorded by the *Stamford Mercury*, was also reported word for word by the *Grantham Journal*.

The reporting of the appearance of the three land workers who had encountered Selina Stanhope sitting against the bridge on the Langtoft road was slightly different from the version recorded in the

Stamford Mercury. In the *Grantham Journal* version, it was Joseph Cook rather than James Jackson, who took centre stage in court. Perhaps understandably, there is some difference as to which of the three men offered Selina Stanhope a ride back to Langtoft: in the earlier version, it was James Jackson; in the later version, it was Joseph Cook. In the final analysis, it hardly mattered, but the more expansive deposition of Joseph Cook, strangely loquacious in comparison with the version reported in the *Stamford Mercury*, recorded a different version of the key incident.

Joseph Cook agreed that he had heard James Jackson tell Selina Stanhope not to hurt the baby, but could not recall hearing him tell her that 'it will perhaps get you a bit of bread when you can't get one' – all he had said was, 'Come on Lina, and ride'.

More significantly, it was Mr Cook's perception that there was nothing about the way Selina Stanhope was sitting by the bridge or what she had said to arouse his suspicion. He had seen her basket about a yard away from where she was sitting, but had not been able to see what was in it.

The *Stamford Mercury* had abruptly concluded its report on the adjourned inquest by referring to evidence heard in court which corroborated other depositions, but chose to leave it unreported. The *Grantham Journal* included the missing testimonies which helped to create a fuller picture of the events of

Friday 18th July, but did not in every respect support the assertion that they corroborated other depositions.

Olive Green, daughter of Langtoft labourer, Thomas Green, deposed that she had seen Selina Stanhope on the evening of Friday, 18th July, between 7 and 8 'clock, as she was on her way home from Market Deeping. She had been sitting against Langtoft Bridge and was nursing a baby. Olive Green had continued walking, apparently passing by without speaking, and had arrived back home at about 8 o'clock.

An hour later, at around 9 o'clock, Olive Green was standing in the doorway of her father's house when Selina Stanhope passed by. Again, she did not speak to her, but she noticed that the bottom of her dress was very wet. She heard a certain Elizabeth Deacon say to her at the time, 'Oh Lina, where have you been to, your dress is very wet?' To which she replied that she had come across the fields. Olive Green said that she did not know whether the grass was wet or not that evening.

She further deposed that when Selina Stanhope passed through the village she did not have a child with her nor had she seen the child when she spotted her by the bridge, although she had heard it cry. Possibly in response to a question in the courtroom to establish clear timelines, Olive Green thought that the walk from the bridge to her house would take about twenty minutes.

The report did not establish who Elizabeth Deacon was, despite her being called to provide a deposition which verified the statement made by Olive Green concerning the suspicious wet dress worn by Selina Stanhope on her return from the bridge. She too had seen Selina Stanhope on the evening of Friday, 18th July, around 9 o'clock, as she walked towards the house of Elizabeth Dobney. She had been asked by Selina Stanhope if she had a barrow which she might borrow, but was refused on the grounds that hers was broken. As they parted company, Elizabeth Deacon noticed that she was wearing a wet dress and asked how it had happened: as deposed by Olive Green, she explained the dress being wet because she had come home across the fields.

Whilst there is no information reported concerning the identity of Elizabeth Deacon, the 1871 Census for Langtoft records an Elizabeth Deacon, born in 1860, living with her large, well established family, whose head was an agricultural labourer by the name of William Deacon. The information does not appear to have been made public during the course of the various court appearances, but Selina Stanhope, illegitimate daughter of Frances Stanhope, is recorded in the *Baptismal Register* of 22nd June, 1856, as Selina Deacon Stanhope. It would seem reasonable to suppose that Selina Stanhope was related, albeit indirectly, to Elizabeth Deacon.

The final additional deposition was from Sarah Fowler, who was recalled by the coroner to give evidence about the suspicious wet dress. Mrs Fowler was quite insistent that when Selina Stanhope turned up at the house her dress was not wet. Perhaps by way of proving that her observation was to be trusted, she gave very precise information that the first time she knocked at the door in a state of near collapse, she was wearing a rather light dress; on her second visit, later that evening, she was wearing a black dress. The change of dress, however, may have signified something more uncomfortable about Selina Stanhope.

Hearing before Major William Parker at Bourne Magistrates' Court concerning the wilful murder of William Stanhope by Selina Stanhope, Tuesday 29th July

Both the *Stamford Mercury* and the *Grantham Journal* ended their lengthy accounts of the coroner's inquest into the death of William Stanhope with a brief paragraph. It was noted that after the Guilty verdict was passed in Market Deeping, Selina Stanhope was brought before Major William Parker JP in Bourne and was subsequently committed to the Lincoln County prison to await trial at the Winter Assizes.

The *Stamford Mercury*'s paragraph was spare in its presentation of the information; the *Grantham*

Journal was slightly more expansive, informing its readers that the evidence presented at the hearing was similar to that heard at the inquest. Perhaps in an attempt to whet the appetite for the trial at the Assizes, the report mentioned that in response to the magistrate a defiant or a resigned Selina Stanhope had stated that 'she had nothing to say'.

The *Lincolnshire Chronicle* published 1st August showed only a passing interest in the Selina Stanhope case, condensed into a bare, extended paragraph which was squeezed without a headline between two other news stories from the Deepings area. The brief report of the resumed inquest merely summarised the detective work of Superintendent Pawson in Derby and the subsequent sentence of Guilty by the coroner's court.

The seeming lack of interest by the Lincoln newspaper is in contrast to a curious report, at times bordering on the bizarre, published on 2nd August in the *Derbyshire Times*.

The article provided the reader with essentials of the case, and occasionally with some interesting hitherto unreported details related to a supposed romantic liaison. It was clear from the outset, however, that the writer was more interested in comparing the events which had taken place in Langtoft with incidents in the novels of Charles Dickens and George Eliot than he was in reporting the due process of law.

The misfortunes of Selina Stanhope were compared to those of Little Emily in *David Copperfield* and Hetty Sorrel in *Adam Bede*; perhaps even more unlikely than these two references was the comparison of a scene from the Langtoft murder story to the pathetic narrative painting, *The Return of the Penitent*, by Luke Fildes, which was currently on show at the Royal Academy.

According to the reporter, the reader would feel compassion for the plight of the two literary unfortunates, but the life story of Selina Stanhope emerging from the inquest was 'perhaps too vulgar in its details to evoke sympathy'. However, her sorry position might at least remind the reader of the two stories, as well as 'the powerful picture' by Fildes. Coming close to evoking pity for the poetically described 'young girl of only three and twenty summers' who was apprehended in Derby for the murder of her child, the writer took the moral high ground. 'It is the same old story', he advised the reader: the child was illegitimate and the man who had 'brought this little life of trouble' had escaped his responsibilities. At this point, the article recounts the story of Selina Stanhope who had arrived in Derby with her child 'some weeks ago' and had made the acquaintance of a man who objected to the child. In response, she had returned home to her father, where she was received 'as Luke Fildes' penitent was received'.

The writer clinched his point with a further display of his cultural prowess by quoting, unacknowledged, a couple of lines from Lord Byron's narrative poem, *The Giaour- a Fragment of a Turkish Tale*:

> *For every woe a tear may claim*
> *Except an erring sister's shame.*

Having been rejected, the 'bare shelter' of the workhouse was her only alternative, but she left 'after a few days experience of a pauper's life', which led to the drowning of her child, just as Hetty Sorrell murdered 'the child of her shame'.

After providing a glimpse of the pathetic beauty of Victorian narrative painting and a brief excursion into the exotic world of poetic Orientalism, the writer ended his article by returning to the rather more prosaic world of Derby. After the killing of her child, Selina Stanhope had walked to the city 'in search of the man with whom she might live', only to be arrested by the police. She was now waiting to be tried, again like Hetty Sorrell, 'for the awful crime of child-murder'.

The story of the romantic connections of Selina Stanhope with a man in Derby seems more convenient to the rhetorical intentions of the article than a factually correct account of her life: walking over sixty miles to Derby seems somewhat implausible, even in a story of romantic desperation.

Trial of Selina Stanhope at the Nottinghamshire and Lincolnshire Assizes, in front of Justice Robert Lush, for the wilful murder of William Stanhope, Monday 9th November, 1879

If the *Lincolnshire Chronicle* had shown scant interest in the unfolding story of the Langtoft murder in its early stages, its reporting of the trial and reprieve on 14th November more than made up for that initial lack of interest.

The Winter Assizes for Nottinghamshire and Lincolnshire, held at the Shire Hall in Nottingham, opened for business purposes on Friday, 6th November, beginning with the swearing in of the County Grand Jury, which comprised of the following gentlemen:

F C Smith MP (Foreman)
T H D Bayley
G Beaumont
J H Becher
E S P Burnell
W T Cuckson
J L Ffytche
A Heymann
R M Knowles
E J Lowe
J H Manners-Sutton

W Need
Joseph Paget
C Seeley Jr
H Sherbrooke
W Sherbrooke
Charles Storer
J W Thackeray
J Thorpe
W Tidmas
W Warrand
W F Webb

The opening address by Justice Lush reminded the Grand Jury that in their deliberations they were representing the counties of both Nottinghamshire and Lincolnshire. However, it was a slightly unusual gaol delivery in that there were no cases related to Nottinghamshire. This 'perfect blank' was in contrast to a number of offences committed in Lincolnshire, including 'a very gross charge against a young woman of wilfully murdering her illegitimate child'. The judge was reassuring, and confidently suggested that the case would not present any difficulties in deciding whether a true bill should be found.

The judge outlined the case of Selina Stanhope to the jury which, if accurately reported, was highly selective in its focus and, on several occasions, either misleading or inaccurate. The prisoner had entered the workhouse with her seven month old child, having previously been living at home 'with her father, but no mother, the father having re-married'. That the father with whom she had been living was her stepfather seemed to have escaped Robert Lush's attention. What also seemed to have escaped his attention were the domestic tensions and pressures which Selina Stanhope had encountered when living with her step-parents in Langtoft, culminating in her eviction on the day of the alleged murder. According to the judge, he could not find 'any trace of discord in family affairs which would cause her to leave home'. It was an astonishing declaration in that evidence of serious domestic discord had been heard in the coroner's court from Elizabeth Dobney, who had made no attempt to disguise her dislike of Selina Stanhope.

The advice to the jury continued with the information that Selina Stanhope had only stayed in the workhouse for a few weeks, before leaving with her child, which at the time was perfectly healthy. The vagueness of the chronology of her stay in the Bourne workhouse was complemented by a similarly unhelpful description of what happened after having left it. According to Justice Lush, Selina Stanhope 'in the course of a day or two went away with the child and came back without it'. The imprecise chronology contrasts with the exact date of her leaving the workhouse deposed by Edwin Jenner at the inquest, which left no doubt about its relationship to the date of alleged murder.

Worse was to follow in that Justice Lush advised the jury that when challenged about the whereabouts of the child, Selina Stanhope had claimed that she had put it out to nurse and had named the persons involved. Unfortunately, the name of these persons was never actually mentioned in any previous deposition nor did it ever emerge during the trial. The error of the judge's claim was matched in its ineptitude by what followed, stating categorically that on the day of her leaving the workhouse she was seen sitting on the river bank and 'shortly after that time' the child was found drowned.

What he did get right was that the child was found naked and that its clothes were found in the prisoner's box.

By any standards, the introductory summary of the evidence suggesting that a true bill should be found, was at best clumsy, at worst, incompetent. Rather than being a secure exposition of the facts expected from a such an eminent judge, it seemed more like the product of a rushed reading of the depositions during his train journey to Nottingham – either that, it was a case of wildly inaccurate reporting by the newspaper.

The trial of Selina Stanhope for her life began as clumsily as the summary of the case heard on the previous Friday. In response to the Clerk of the Arraigns, she had replied that she was Guilty. At this point, the judge seemed to have been taken by surprise, and reminded Selina Stanhope that she was on trial for the murder of a child. On her behalf, William Linton, the Governor of Nottingham prison, told the court that Selina Stanhope wished to withdraw the plea as she was now defended. In response to this development, Justice Lush asked the prisoner if she had employed any gentleman to defend her in court? It seemed a somewhat strange question addressed to a woman who had recently been admitted to the workhouse as a destitute pauper. It should have come as no surprise that Selina Stanhope had not employed a gentleman to defend her.

An apparent solution to the problem was Justice Lush requesting Mr Gilbert George Kennedy to defend the prisoner. Perhaps Selina Stanhope, at this point, might have felt a sense of hope, as well as gratitude to both Justice Lush and Mr Kennedy, but such short notice to prepare a convincing defence of a woman who seemed to have committed the indefensible, and had already admitted to it, seemed a tall order for any legal Counsel. It was perhaps even more of a tall order for Gilbert George Kennedy than most, whose undistinguished legal career until 1888, when he was made Recorder of Grantham, seemed to consist mainly of the humdrum work of a Revising

Barrister and the occasional appearance at the Lincoln Quarter Sessions. Thirty-five year old Mr Kennedy, as with Edward Chandos Leigh who had defended Lucy Ann Buxton, was more distinguished as a sportsman than as a man of law, having played football for the Wanderers at Crystal Palace in 1866 and for a Scotland XI against England at the Kennington Oval in 1870, in addition to having served on the English FA Cup Committee between 1869 and 1870. His two contributions to theoretical jurisprudence, *The Law of Land Drainage and Sewers*, published in 1884, and *A Guide to the Coal Mines Regulation Act, 1887*, published in 1888, perhaps indicate where his legal talents lay.

Opening the case for the Prosecution, Mr Edmund Lumley insisted that the facts of the case were 'very short and simple': he simply recapitulated the essentials of the case, although the newspaper did not report them.

The first witness to appear was Edwin Jenner, who repeated his deposition from the inquest at the coroner's court, but in addition provided further information about Selina Stanhope's short stay in the workhouse. On admission, she had stated that she was a single woman and that the child, named William, was her own. At the time, she was still 'partly' suckling the child. She had left the workhouse at her own request, holding the child, who was dressed in a plaid shawl and a coloured frock and hood: the red and black plaid shawl shown in court he believed to be the same shawl. He also deposed that he had confirmed the dead child's identity at the White Horse Inn at Market Deeping, on Wednesday the 23rd July. Under cross-examination from Mr Kennedy, Jenner told the court that Selina Stanhope had been admitted under the Relieving Officer's order as a pauper, and that she was quiet and well-behaved during her time in the workhouse. He also affirmed that she was kind to the child and he was not aware that her mind was affected in any way. Justice Lush had it reiterated by Jenner that the mother had been affectionate towards her son.

Elizabeth Dobney confirmed to the court that Selina Stanhope was the daughter of her husband's first wife and that she had lived with them when she wasn't in domestic service. About a fortnight before 26th June, she had arrived at her house with a child of about seven months old. The deposition seemed to suggest that the existence of the child was a complete surprise to her; what she also made abundantly clear, was that Selina Stanhope had gone to the Bourne workhouse on 26th June 'of her own accord'. She had left Bourne after three weeks, but did not say why she had returned to Langtoft. Further, she left the house the following day, between 6 and 7 o'clock in the evening, taking the child with her, but did not say where or why she was going. Mrs Dobney also mentioned, in passing, that she 'previously walked out very little with the child'.

On her return between 8 and 9 o'clock without the child, she had asked where it was and was told that it was with a nurse in Towngate, although she did not say at whose house, nor did she ask. The prisoner took her box away in a wheelbarrow to Reedman's, the coal merchant, the location where articles were deposited for carriers to collect. She returned after an hour, had her tea and slept the night in the house before departing the following morning: she did not come back.

To some extent, the deposition of Mrs Dobney repeated the evidence heard at the coroner's inquest. However, the fresh information, underlined the domestic difficulties between the two women and also a degree of defensiveness in Mrs Dobney's insistence that Selina Stanhope and her child had not ended up in the workhouse as a result of any pressure from her.

The continuation of her deposition provided further evidence, not recorded at the inquest, which perhaps went some way to explaining how Inspector Pawson was able to confirm the identity of the dead boy so quickly. On the morning of Tuesday, 22nd July, Mrs Dobney 'had occasion' to pass the division drain between Langtoft and Market Deeping, and saw the police inspector pulling the body out of the water: it was a remarkable coincidence which enabled her to identify the naked child as Selina Stanhope's. Equally remarkable, if the report is accurate, it appears that no conversation between the police inspector and the witness took place, despite her being close enough to observe the identity of the dead child.

Under cross-examination by Mr Kennedy, small details emerged which were only perhaps hinted at during the inquest in Market Deeping and further indicated domestic disharmony. On being asked where Selina Stanhope had been living before she returned home with a child, she replied that she did not know, adding rather tetchily that she 'did not ask'. Not for the first time in her deposition, Mrs Dobney made it clear that she had preferred not to get involved in her stepdaughter's life. In response to further questioning, she told the court that she did not know how long Selina's mother and stepfather had been married; more significantly, she mentioned that when Selina had returned home Mr Dobney was ill and he had told her that 'he could do without her'. She also confirmed that her husband had recently died.

The report of the deposition of Joseph Cook was memorable not so much for what he told the court, which was essentially a very short version of his encounter with Selina Stanhope at the bridge outlined at the inquest, but rather for the apparent confusions of the reporter. Whilst all the accounts of the inquest found in the various newspapers record the three land workers who spoke to Selina Stanhope as being James Jackson, Joseph Cook and Henry Bell, the trial reporter seemed to invent a new agricultural labourer by the name of Henry Dobney to replace Henry Bell. His apparent mistake was compounded by the reporter helpfully alerting the reader to the fact that Henry Dobney was not the stepfather of Selina Stanhope – a mistake difficult to make when her stepfather was called Thomas. If the reporter's hearing or understanding were a possible problem in the recording of names, his knowledge of the local topography of Deeping Fens let him down further when he renamed Nidd's Bridge as Nidge Bridge.

The only interesting difference between what Joseph Cook deposed at the Coroner's court and what he said at the trial was that whilst talking to Selina Stanhope he had 'noticed something bulky in her arms, over which she was leaning'.

Perhaps the passage of time had reshaped his memory.

Olive Green, the next witness, also seemed to struggle to produce a consistent recollection of what she had seen on the evening of Friday, 18th July. At the inquest, she had said that she had seen Selina Stanhope at the bridge and that she was nursing a baby; in her latest version of events, she had seen her, but could not say for definite that she was holding a child, although under cross-examination, probably prompted by Mr Lumley, she recalled that she had heard the crying of a child. Olive Green confirmed that as she stood talking with Elizabeth Deacon, she had noticed that Selina Stanhope's dress was wet.

In terms of a replication of a previously heard deposition, Elizabeth Fowler was probably the most reliable witness to be heard, although the events she recounted were compressed into one visit on the evening of 18th July, rather than two. She re-told the story of Selina Stanhope arriving at the house between 8 and 9 o'clock in the evening in a distressed state and of her being offered food and drink. She also recounted the exchange concerning the whereabouts of the child, the reassurances of Selina Stanhope and her intentions to send money for its upkeep once she had settled in Derby. The only addition to the inquest deposition was that the prisoner had asked to borrow a barrow, but Mrs Fowler was unable to help as she did not have one: however, she did hear a barrow being pushed past her house later that evening.

Her reported final sentence seemed to capture the essence of Selina Stanhope's melancholy story: 'Witness told her to go home, and she said she had no home'.

The following deposition was from William Holmes which like his previous testimonies was a flat, fact-filled and emotionally detached recollection of finding a dead body, not touching it, informing the police and taking it to the White Horse Inn. Interestingly, there was no mention of Elizabeth Dobney luckily passing by the drain to identify the body.

Inspector Thomas Pawson took up the narrative from the point where William Holmes ended, recounting that he had gone to Nidd's Bridge accompanied by the local farmer and had found the body of the dead child, lying on its right side. With police precision, he described the ghastly discovery in detail: the head was a little lower than the feet and resting upon the bottom of the drain. He had taken the body out of the drain and examined it for any marks of violence, but had found none. He had looked for footprints close to where the child was found and discovered a mark where a person had possibly slipped into the water; whilst the grass was trodden down, there was no distinct footprint.

This was followed by an account of his trip to Derby on the same day and arriving at the house of a Mrs Mary Ann Clayton of Bridge Gate, where he found Selina Stanhope in the sitting room. His description of his interview with the prisoner reported by the newspaper was an interesting amalgam of the two different versions of events allegedly heard at the inquest and reported in the *Stamford Mercury* and the *Grantham Journal*.

This third version of the inspector's interview with the suspect was brisk: he asked her if she was from Langtoft in Lincolnshire and if she had had an illegitimate child? To both questions Selina Stanhope had answered in the affirmative. After cautioning her as to what she might say, he charged her with 'murdering her illegitimate child by drowning it in a ditch near Nidge Bridge (*sic*), in the parish of Langtoft.' After the precipitous formalities were over, Inspector Pawson asked to see her box which was searched in her presence. He discovered the items of clothing then on view in court, with the exception of the hood, which was found in another part of the premises by Detective Clarke. The triumphant discovery of key evidence for the prosecution of a crime after the suspect had allegedly been formally charged with that crime, seemed a possible weakness in the case against Selina Stanhope, which the Counsel for the Defence might have exploited in his summing up.

Before being cross-examined, the inspector completed his deposition by repeating first Selina Stanhope's insistence that she had intended to send the clothes on to the people in Market Deeping who were looking after her child, and then her confession, on the way back to Bourne, that she had committed the crime. In this version of the deposition, as reported by the *Lincolnshire Chronicle*, the confession took place on the train from Derby to Bourne and that Selina Stanhope was in some distress.

The inspector's responses to being cross-examined related to the place where William Stanhope had died. He gave a more precise set of measurements concerning the depth of the water in which the body was found, as well as the shape and the height of the culvert beneath the road. The reporter does not identify who asked the question, however, so it is difficult assess the relevance of the information. Similarly, his final words, assuring the court that on arresting Selina Stanhope he had told her that her child had been found and identified, it is difficult to work out the relevance of the statement without knowing who had asked the question . On the surface, it appears to be a question from the Counsel for the Defence possibly relating to police protocols, but without further evidence it remains speculative and if important, might have been queried further, either during the deposition or the summing up by Mr Kennedy.

The final witness for the Prosecution was William Deacon, the surgeon who had performed the post mortem at the inquest. He repeated his conclusion that the child had died by drowning, adding details from the post mortem examination which were not in any reports of the inquest. The contents of the boy's stomach were a mixture of mother's milk, water, a few pieces of mud and very minute pieces of grass, leading to the conclusion that he must have been alive when placed in the water: if he had been dead, 'there would be no power of swallowing'.

The only reported answer made by the doctor to an implied question, was that he had previous experience of dealing with cases of drowning. If asked by the Counsel for the Prosecution, it was clearly meant to confirm the expertise of Mr Deacon; if asked by the Counsel for the Defence in a possible attempt to undermine the reliability of medical opinion, it would have seemed peculiarly inept, given Mr Deacon's many years of experience in conducting post mortems in an area defined by water and drainage systems.

After the statement of Selina Stanhope that she had nothing to say was 'put in', Mr Lumley summarised the case against the prisoner in three watertight nutshells. William Stanhope could not have been suffocated before being put into the dyke; neither could he have fallen into the dyke, as the evidence showed that the child was naked; and finally, the mother had been found to be in possession of the child's clothes.

It was 'pretty conclusive', Mr Lumley suggested, that the prisoner was guilty of drowning her own child.

Counsel for the Defence's challenge, in the face of the evidence, was to save his client from the hangman:

the fact that she had confessed to the crime made any plea of innocence redundant, but a virtuoso performance from Mr Kennedy might sway the jury to recommend mercy, should there be sufficient grounds to do so.

The opening gambit of the Counsel was to insist that this was a case which should 'excite commiseration' and that the jury should not feel anything other than sympathy for the prisoner and the circumstances in which she had found herself.

Had the young woman, a pauper, a home to go to, he suggested, then things might have turned out differently for her. Her stepfather, he reminded the jury, had been 'vexed' when she came to his house, and she was left to walk five or six miles to the workhouse in Bourne, 'without an attempt being made to restrain her'. She had told Mrs Fowler that she had no home, and that was the feeling she had when she set off on that 'fatal evening', from which journey she came back, but without the child.

The construction of an image of cruel rejection and isolation was clearly Mr Kennedy's intent.

Having followed an emotive line of defence, however, he then appeared to divert to a more generalised and predictable argument, which was that there was no conclusive evidence as to what had happened at the side of the bridge that evening: all the evidence which the jury had before them was conjecture and 'it was on conjecture alone' they were being asked to say that the prisoner had wilfully killed her child by drowning it.

It was a line of argument which was part of the stock in trade of all Defence Counsels, which sometimes worked, but perhaps was hardly worth the mention in this case, when the weight of evidence, including the prisoner's own admission of culpability, was so strong. At this point, there is a sense of a professional exercise in defending a hopeless case, rather than the serious construction of an irresistible argument for a Not Guilty verdict, or more realistically, a strong recommendation for mercy.

Returning to what he perhaps thought would be safer and more realistic ground, Mr Kennedy, highlighted the fact that all the depositions had concurred that Selina Stanhope had been affectionate towards her child. To some extent, this was true, but an alert jury might have recalled the uneasiness of James Jackson at the bridge when he warned her not to harm the child, as well as the unpleasant jibe from Elizabeth Dobney, only slightly less caustic than the one voiced at the inquest perhaps, which suggested that Selina Stanhope 'walked out very little with the child'. Possibly more telling was Mr Kennedy's observation that the medical evidence had shown that she had breastfed the child that night. 'Could they consistently believe', he asked, 'that a mother could suckle her child one moment and wilfully murder it the next?'

It was a neatly constructed rhetorical question, but possibly fell between the two stools of defending Selina Stanhope on a capital crime on the one hand, and trying to persuade a jury to extend human sympathy to beyond the strict letter of the law, on the other.

That Mr Kennedy was short on convincing ideas was suggested by him next voicing the possibility that Selina Stanhope, in her distressed condition, had accidentally smothered the child whilst breast feeding it: 'she may have pressed it too close to her bosom, suffocated it, and would have been powerless to help it'. Realising that the child was dead on her lap and 'knowing that she had no home or friend', she decided 'to bury the body and her shame in that dyke'. To avoid the child being recognised, she had removed its clothes and then told people that she had put it out to nurse.

As a rhetorical exercise in synthesising diverse inconvenient elements of a case into a coherent whole, it was ingenious; as a plausible, clinching explanation of the death by drowning of a small child, it was ludicrous.

The summing up by Mr Kennedy ended with a direct appeal to the jury for their merciful consideration of the prisoner, 'who not only was without the support of the father of the child, whoever he was, but was friendless and homeless'.

Before summing up the case, according to the *Lincolnshire Chronicle*, Justice Lush recalled William Deacon, who said that in his opinion, William Stanhope had been dead in the water for three or four days; and also Mrs Dobney, who deposed that the prisoner's young brother had gone with her when she left the house with her box, but had later returned.

In summarising the case, Robert Lush suggested to the jury that it was a sad one, which would elicit their sympathy; however, it was also one which required them to use sound judgement. The central questions were whether the child had drowned and if so, was it as a result of a wilful intention to murder? The judge was quite clear that in his opinion the evidence 'was very complete' and that 'there was no dispute about it in the slightest degree'.

More sympathetically, Robert Lush reminded the jury that the young woman had neither a father nor a mother, only a stepfather who was ill - a labourer unable to work, who had a second wife 'earning what she could by working in the fields'. Selina Stanhope had come home with an illegitimate child and the jury could not be surprised by the stepfather being angry that she had 'brought that encumbrance upon him', nor by her not having been given a very warm reception at the house. This had led her 'to desire to leave home' and find refuge in the workhouse, and there she might have remained had she not left on 17th July, having given the usual twenty-four hour notice.

In conclusion, the jury had to decide upon the two key issues which he had outlined earlier in his summary.

The jury took only a short time to reach a verdict of Guilty, but with a strong recommendation for mercy.

Having assumed the black cap and whilst Selina Stanhope was reportedly 'sobbing bitterly at intervals', he addressed her directly. To his mind, the jury had reached the correct decision as she was undoubtedly guilty of murder; the jury had also made a strong recommendation for mercy, which he would take forward to the relevant quarters. Within his terms of office, he could do no more than pronounce the death sentence and instruct that she be taken to Lincoln, to be hanged and then buried within the precincts of the prison. The jury had given her some hope of a reprieve from the consequences of her 'most grievous sin', but meanwhile, he hoped she would join her prayers with his, 'that God may have mercy on you'.

Unconsoled by the pious platitudes, it seems, Selina Stanhope was taken down 'loudly sobbing'.

The same account of the trial, word for word, was

published on the same day by the *Nottinghamshire Guardian*.

A different report on the trial was published in the *Stamford Mercury* on 14th November, the same day as the *Lincolnshire Chronicle* and the *Nottingham Guardian*, with the headline 'Infanticide at Langtoft – Sentence of Death'.

The style of reporting in the Stamford newspaper was less formal and structured than that of the Lincoln newspaper, resulting in an occasional loss of clarity as to whether it was the Counsel for the Prosecution who was presenting the facts of the case or a witness who had been called to the stand and was repeating a previous deposition or the reporter summarising the evidence. A reader familiar with the case from the earlier extensive reports on the pre-trial inquest would have been able to make sense of the various threads, but anyone coming to the story of Selina Stanhope's misfortunes for the first time might have struggled to disentangle the more complex narrative strands.

In most respects, the account of the trial in the *Stamford Mercury* reflected that of the *Lincolnshire Chronicle*, but occasionally added hitherto unreported information which provided either a better understanding of the case or prompted questions concerning the narratives constructed at Market Deeping and reported from the Nottingham courtroom by the Lincoln newspaper.

As a preamble to the unfolding courtroom drama of child murder in Langtoft, the newspaper provided some very interesting background information on the life of Selina Stanhope, possibly voiced by the Counsel for the Prosecution in his opening remarks on the case. The prisoner's father and mother were both dead and she had been in domestic service in Derby. The continuation of the narrative is very precise in its mapping out of the subsequent key events of her life: about eleven months previous, she had left her situation in Derby 'on account of her being enceinte' and had returned to her stepfather's house in Langtoft, 'where she was confined of the child she is charged with murdering'.

To a contemporary reader, the story of a female domestic servant losing their position after becoming pregnant would have been an all too familiar one, as would the father of the child remaining either elusive or a complete mystery.

On 20th June, Selina Stanhope was admitted to the Bourne Union Workhouse as a destitute pauper, as her stepfather and his wife 'gave her to understand that they could not keep her and her child any longer'.

If correct, the story of Selina Stanhope's return to Langtoft seemed to be at variance with that deposed by Elizabeth Dobney reported in the *Lincolnshire Chronicle*, which gave the impression that the existence of William Stanhope was a complete surprise to her when she turned up at the house in early June 'with an infant child'. It also contradicted Mrs Dobney's insistence that Selina Stanhope had not gone to the workhouse under any kind of pressure from her, but of her own accord.

Whilst on the whole, the report of the trial in the *Stamford Mercury* does not radically depart from the version in the *Lincolnshire Chronicle* in terms of the key events which took place immediately before and after the alleged murder of William Stanhope, its account of the summing up by the learned counsels differs a good deal.

The account of the summing up by Mr Lumley in the *Lincolnshire Chronicle* created a sense of a neatly packaged speech of straightforward interpretations of the facts of the case for the jury to consider, all of them leading to the inevitable conclusion that Selina Stanhope was guilty. Its pared down simplicity seemed to suggest that any alternative ways of looking at the evidence were either not worth considering or non-existent.

The more expansive account of Mr Lumley's summary found in the *Stamford Mercury* indicates that he was prepared to seriously address arguments put forward by Mr Kennedy, despite his position being secure. After having summed up the 'chief parts of the evidence', he confidently asserted that the fact that water mixed with grass and mud had been found in the victim's stomach 'entirely negatived' the anticipated theory for the Defence, which he presumed his learned colleague would be presenting to the jury in his summing up. There were clearly no unpleasant surprises anticipated from the Counsel for the Defence, as Mr Lumley referred to the possibility, emerging from what he had observed during the cross examination of witnesses, that William Stanhope might have been suffocated by his mother's breasts or suffered 'a sudden fit of croup'.

His final words were part of the ritual politeness of courtroom etiquette, although there is perhaps a sense of genuine sentiment beyond the formulaic emptiness. Mr Lumley suggested that the jury would be only too glad if they could gather from his learned friend anything which might lead to finding the accused guilty of a lesser crime than murder or even acquit her altogether. The latter was unlikely, as was a verdict of manslaughter, but it may have given some encouragement to the jury in terms of a strong recommendation for mercy. It is perhaps no surprise that Mr Lumley was to later add his name to a petition to save Selina Stanhope from the hangman.

The account of the summing up by the Counsel for the Defence was also more extensive than the version published in the *Lincolnshire Chronicle*, both in terms of emotive rhetoric and alternative hypotheses of death by suffocation.

According to the *Stamford Mercury*, Mr Kennedy 'drew an affecting picture of the unfortunate girl' who had been 'seduced, deserted and compelled to give up her situation'. Her misfortunes continued on her return to the house of her stepfather and stepmother 'where her life was made so wretched' that she sought refuge in the workhouse. Even after leaving the workhouse, a destitute pauper with a small child, and returning to the family home, she was again 'driven forth' after one night's stay by her stepmother, leaving her to seek shelter where she could for herself and the child. Not knowing where to go or 'where to lay her head, she sat down by the roadside weary and sick at heart'. It was a harrowing picture of human misery which, despite its suppression of some of the facts of the case, created a compelling sympathy for the prisoner as a victim of circumstances and other people's malice.

That was the easy bit: the construction of a plausible explanation for the death of a small child, towards which the Counsel for the Defence was quite clearly leading, was not so straightforward. If the argument for an accidental killing recorded in the *Lincolnshire Chronicle* was unconvincing, the expanded version found in the *Stamford Mercury* resembled a desperately improvised fiction.

In her 'great anguish' whilst seated by the roadside, Selina Stanhope 'may have unwittingly pressed her child too close to her breast' and suffocated it. There could be no doubt, Mr Kennedy admitted, that the child had died from suffocation, but there were many different ways in which a child might die from suffocation, including the one he had suggested, 'or even by a sudden paroxysm of croup'.

Unsurprisingly, the suggestion of a sudden blockage of the airways which, as reported by the newspaper, had the feel of an afterthought, was not expanded upon. Instead, he returned to the emotive image of Selina Stanhope, whom he characterised as 'evidently not of strong mind' and described as 'being frightened to go back home or anywhere else with her dead child lest she be charged with murdering it'. The report in the *Stamford Mercury*, at this point, went on to duplicate the unlikely story of the young mother seeking to hide the dead body and her shame by throwing it into the water, which was also published in the *Lincolnshire Chronicle*. If the reader of either of the newspapers at this point felt that the Counsel for the Defence was testing credulity to breaking point, the continuation recorded only in the Stamford newspaper, certainly confirmed it. In a futile attempt to face the inconvenient facts of the post mortem head on, Mr Kennedy explained away the presence of grass and mud in the stomach of the dead child with the feeble suggestion that the mother had given the child a drink of water from the dyke.

His outlandish special pleading concluded, the Counsel for the Defence completed his work with the less imaginative request that the jury might give Selina Stanhope the benefit of any doubts they may have about her guilt, reminding them that the case against her was built entirely on conjecture.

The summing up by Justice Lush reported in the *Lincolnshire Chronicle* contained a good deal of comment which illustrated his contention that the case, like all such cases, was a very painful one. His summing up, as reported in the *Stamford Mercury*, was less overt in its sympathies, focusing more upon the unarguable weight of evidence against the prisoner and the need for the jury, as men of reason, to exercise sound judgment, rather than be swayed by natural human sympathy. The final observation made by Robert Lush was unarguable: the prisoner had confessed to the crime.

Without leaving the box, the jury reached a verdict of Guilty, but with the strong recommendation for mercy, on account of the prisoner's age and the destitute condition in which she had found herself when the child was drowned.

The death sentence was passed with the reassurance that the recommendation of the jury would be forwarded as the beginning of the process of a possible reprieve.

Selina Stanhope, perhaps worn down and out

by the threat of an ignominious ending to a life yet barely lived, 'moaned piteously' on hearing her fate and had to be supported from the dock.

Reprieve of Selina Stanhope from the Death Sentence, received by the Governor of Lincoln County Prison, 25th November, 1879

A number of accounts of the submission of a petition to the Home Secretary to reprieve Selina Stanhope were reported in the Lincolnshire popular press, each with their own particular emphasis.

A glib paragraph, culled from London's *Daily News*, was published in the *Boston Guardian* on 21st November, and alerted the reader to the organisation of a memorial for Selina Stanhope in Lincoln, which had been 'influentially signed', but said little else.

A more informed and informative notice was published on the same day by the *Lincolnshire Chronicle*, which praised the efforts of Mr John Giles of Guildhall Street, Lincoln, who had set the petition process in motion 'with commendable zeal'. It was noted also that he had involved himself on other occasions with 'similarly situated prisoners'. The report did not mention any names, but Mr Giles had also been a key force in organising a petition for the reprieve of Emma Wade just six months earlier.

The Lincoln butcher, as part of his strategy, had

also contacted Edward Chaplin, MP for Lincoln, 'with a view to the Home Secretary being urged to pass upon the poor woman the lightest possible sentence compatible with the offence of which she has been convicted'.

The report was a celebration of local initiative, but it was also careful to point out that the newspaper did not support the complete abolition of capital punishment, as there were crimes which were 'of such a diabolical character that death appears to be the only adequate punishment'. However, there were cases of murder whose circumstances justified the use of the Royal Prerogative: the case of Selina Stanhope was, by general consent, such a case.

The newspaper, perhaps buoyed by the city's part in the reprieve of Emma Wade, was optimistic that the strong recommendation for mercy by the jury, backed up by a memorial from both Lincoln and Langtoft, would be favourably received by the Home Office.

The memorial petition had already been signed by the mayor, all the magistrates, most of the Town Council and many of Lincoln's leading citizens. By way of practical advice, the report concluded by assuring its readers that it would be available for signing at the shop of Mr Giles until that evening, Friday, 21ST November, before it was forwarded to London.

On the following day, the *Grantham Journal* published details of a memorial and petition being organised at Langtoft, which the *Lincolnshire Chronicle* had mentioned briefly in passing. The annexed petition had been 'signed with great eagerness' in the village in the hope it would contribute to the remission of 'the unfortunate young woman'.

Helpfully, and unusually, the newspaper was able to publish the complete text of the memorial being sent to Richard Assheton Cross for his consideration, which presented reasons why she might be reprieved:

> *We the undersigned, the minister, church-wardens, and the parishioners of the parish of Langtoft, Lincolnshire, desire to bring under your notice the case of Selina Stanhope, now lying under sentence of death for the crime of infanticide lately committed in this parish, and trusting Her Majesty may be induced to commute the said penalty for such lesser punishment as may be seen fitting. Selina Stanhope is an orphan, without any home, and had not the advantage of proper early training, and we believe that desperation of her state led her to commit the crime of which she has been found guilty; while, therefore, we acknowledge that such a crime deserves severe punishment, we think that the ends of public justice would be better fulfilled by some*

penalty less than the extreme one of death, and we
hope that et cetera.

Signed the vicar, churchwardens and three
hundred and twenty inhabitants.

The text of the Langtoft memorial had been published the day before by the *Stamford Mercury*, but did not include the opening paragraph found in the *Grantham Journal*, which extolled the overwhelming support for Selina Stanhope in the village.

The newspaper reports on the first stages of petitioning the Home Office to reprieve Selina Stanhope were in due course followed up with the news of her respite from the death sentence, when it was officially confirmed by letters from Adolphus Liddell, the Under-Secretary of State for the Home Office, written on 25th November, just seven days before she was due to be hanged.

The effusive report in the *Lincolnshire Chronicle* made no attempt to hide its delight that the citizens of Lincoln and one of its MPs had made a decisive contribution to saving Selina Stanhope from the hangman's noose. It reminded its readers that Mr John Giles had been 'instrumental in getting up the memorial' and that it had been numerously signed by the mayor, the magistrates, members of the corporation and 'many influential inhabitants of the city'. By way of illustrating the part played by

Lincoln in the story of the respite of the convicted murderer, the newspaper published three important documents for public information: two of them were bureaucratic confirmations of the Home Secretary's decision, whilst the third was a long letter from Edward Chaplin MP which provided fascinating insights into how the reprieve process really worked – as opposed to how people thought it worked.

The first document was an extract from a letter addressed to Major Edward Mackay, the Governor of Lincoln prison, received on Wednesday, 26th November, from the Home Secretary, which confirmed the respite of the death sentence:

> *I am to signify the Queen's commands that the execution of the sentence of death passed upon Selina Stanhope be respited until further signification of Her Majesty's pleasure.*

By the same post, John Giles also received a confirmation of the respite: the letter appeared to be published in full, rather than an extract, written in the same stiff civil servant formulary:

> *Whitehall, 25th November, 1879*
> *The Secretary of State for the Home Department having considered your application on behalf of Selina Stanhope. I am directed to acquaint you that*

he has felt warranted, under all the circumstances,
in advising Her Majesty to respite the capital
sentence in this case.

I am, sir, your obedient servant, A F O Liddell.

If the first two documents were intended to officially confirm the outcome of the Lincoln memorial, the third was published to impress upon the reader the important part that Edward Chaplin MP had played in ensuring that the life of Selina Stanhope was spared by having 'directly interested himself in supporting the prayer of the memorialists'.

The letter, written to John Giles, confirmed the reprieve, but more importantly it described in some detail how Chaplain had used his privileged position to good effect by talking directly to the two most important people involved in making the decision about the case:

25 Charles Street, Berkeley Square, London.
25th November, 1879.
Sir – I had an interview this morning with Mr
Machonochie, the head of the Criminal Department
at the Home Office, and was fortunate enough also
to have an interview with Mr Cross, who was kind
enough to break through an invariable rule of never
seeing any private person in criminal cases, in
consideration of my being member for Lincoln, and

*at my earnest solicitation. I am very pleased to tell
you that Mr Cross has respited the unfortunate girl,
Selina Stanhope, and has ordered the sentence to be
commuted to penal servitude for life. I also strongly
urged upon Mr Cross, the desirability of reducing
this sentence as much as possible, but he told me
that in the first instance there was an invariable rule
that he had never remembered to have departed
from, that in the case of the sentence of death being
respited it was always penal servitude for life. At
the same time, I should have every hope that if at
some future time it should be deemed advisable
to memorialise the Home Secretary for a future
commutation of sentence, he might be inclined to
listen to arguments in its favour.*

To reassure its readers that Lincoln was not
claiming all the credit for the reprieve of Selina
Stanhope, it magnanimously reminded them that
the extensively signed memorial from Langtoft sent
to Whitehall 'would doubtless have had due weight'.
However, at the same time, the newspaper was
compelled to suggest that it would be justified in
expressing 'the obligations of humane people' to Mr
Giles for his 'disinterested labours ' and to Colonel
Chaplin 'for his exertions in the matter'.

Perhaps caught up in the moment of over-
celebration, the report ended optimistically,

expressing the hope that the suggestion of the Lincoln MP would not be forgotten and that in time a new memorial would be sent up to the Home Secretary praying for the release of the unhappy woman from custody.

In the meantime, should she have 'conducted herself in a proper manner during her incarceration', the prayer of such a memorial 'in all probability' would be granted.

On the same day, the *Stamford Mercury* published both of the letters received by John Giles in full and thanked him for having 'kindly taken the matter in hand'. The report also provided the additional information that Mr Giles had also been in contact Charles Seely, Lincoln's other MP, who had 'promised assistance'.

The *Grantham Journal*, on the following day, under the headline 'The Langtoft Child Murder', published a report of the reprieve, peculiarly devoid of any hint of celebration. It recorded that the Governor of the Lincoln County prison had received an official letter of commutation to penal servitude for life and then gave a précis of the final paragraph of Chaplin's letter concerning the possibility of a further reduced sentence at some point in the future.

Interestingly, none of the Lincolnshire newspapers referred to the part played by the city of Nottingham in the reprieve of Selina Stanhope. Whilst she had no connection with the city or the county, her trial had been heard at Nottingham's Shire Hall, and a number of its citizens had served on the jury.

Charles Bradshaw, a local solicitor and the Acting Under-Sheriff for Nottinghamshire had also submitted a memorial to the Home Office on behalf of Selina Stanhope, bearing the signatures of the jury as well as the Prosecuting Counsel.

Documents related to the work of the Nottinghamshire memorialists appeared in the *Correspondence* section of the *Nottingham Evening Post*, published on the 28th November, which had been sent in to the editor of the newspaper by Charles Bradshaw himself. Their presentation for publication was remarkably understated, given Mr Bradshaw's reputation for acrimonious exchanges of letters in Nottingham newspapers, most notoriously in his very public dispute with Christopher Wordsworth, the Bishop of Lincoln, concerning perceived popish irregularities in the parish of St John the Baptist, Leenside, where he was a church warden.

Mr Bradshaw had prepared and sent the memorial to the Home Office and that morning he had received confirmation from the Home Secretary that Selina Stanhope had been reprieved. He now wished to make public the correspondence between himself and the Secretary of State, as well as the memorial sent in support of the young woman:

Copy Correspondence and Memorial

> *County Sheriff's Office, Journal*
> *Chambers, Pelham Street, Nottingham.*
> *25th November, 1879.*
> *The Rt. Hon. R. A. Cross,*
> *Secretary of State,*
> *Home Department, Whitehall.*

Re: Selina Stanhope

Sir – I have been requested by the jurors who tried the above prisoner, who is now lying under sentence of death, and is to be executed at Lincoln on Monday next, to forward to you the enclosed memorial praying a commutation of the sentence.

I remain your obedient servant

Charles Bradshaw, Acting Under-Sheriff

> *To the Right Honourable Secretary of State*
> *for the Home Department.*

The memorial of the undersigned –

Sheweth – That on Monday tenth of November, instant, one Selina Stanhope, a servant, aged twenty-three years, was tried at the Winter Assize, held at the Shire Hall, Nottingham, for the wilful murder of her illegitimate child, William Stanhope, in the parish of Langtoft, in the county of Lincoln, on the 18th day of July last, when, we, the undersigned, being the jury empanelled to try the case, found a verdict of guilty against the said Selena (sic) Stanhope, but strongly recommended her to mercy.

It was elicited from the evidence offered that the prisoner had neither father nor mother, and that in her distress, after the birth of her child, having no home to go to, she sought shelter in the house of her step-father, who had married again, but was vexed at her returning with her child. She then went to the workhouse and remained there for a short time, when she left, and again went to her step-father's to seek her home there. She was, however, received again with unkindness. In her despair she then seems to have put an end to the life of her child.

The evidence all tended to show that the prisoner was uniformly kind in her treatment of the child. It is submitted that the circumstances under which the crime was committed make it a case in which there are strong grounds for extenuation, the evidence tending to show that the deed was not premeditated, but was a sudden frenzy caused by the prisoner's despair at her situation, being without friends, relations or home.

Your petitioners therefore humbly pray you to take into consideration the circumstances of the case and advise her Majesty to extend her clemency by commuting the capital sentence passed on the said Selina Stanhope.

And your petitioners will ever pray et cetera.

JURORS' SIGNATURES:

William Jebb	*Edwin Wilmshurst*
Joseph Metheringham	*William Wood*
Leslie Wm Stephenson	*Samuel Johnson*
Marshall Savidge	*John W Holmes*
James Wood	*Joseph Templeman*
William Richardson	*Joseph Oxley*

E Lumley, Counsel for the prosecution

Whitehall 26th November, 1879

Sir – I am directed by Mr Secretary Cross to acknowledge the receipt of your letter of yesterday's date, forwarding a memorial on behalf of Selina Stanhope and I am to acquaint you that under all circumstances Mr Cross was felt justified in advising her Majesty to respite the capital sentence in this case.

I am, sir, your obedient servant, A. F. O. Liddell

Thanks to the concerted efforts of Langtoft, Lincoln and Nottingham, Selina Stanhope was reprieved, although the earnest optimism of Edward Chaplin that there might soon be yet another local memorial, followed by a further commutation of the sentence, whilst worthy, was ultimately facile. Selina

Stanhope was to spend nearly a decade in Woking prison, before being conditionally discharged into the Elizabeth Fry Refuge in Hackney, on 24th May, 1889, and then later rehabilitated into domestic service in the following November, at the house of William and Mary Vinter, living at 38 Great Percy Street in Pentonville.

She remained in their service until 1897, when she married Thomas Murshed Lamb in West Ham, enjoying a settled anonymous life with him for more than thirty years, but still haunted, no doubt, by the dreadful events which took place in Langtoft, beside a drain, on the evening of Friday, 18th July, 1879.

Appendix One

Key Players in the Selina Stanhope Story

BAYLEY, T H D. Served on the Grand Jury at the trial of Selina Stanhope, at the Shire Hall, Nottingham.

BEAUMONT, G. Served on the Grand Jury at the trial of Selina Stanhope, at the Shire Hall, Nottingham.

BECHER, J H. Served on the Grand Jury at the trial of Selina Stanhope, at the Shire Hall, Nottingham.

BELL, Henry. Agricultural Labourer. Gave evidence at inquest into the death of William Stanhope. Resident of High Street, Langtoft.

BURNELL, E S P. Served on the Grand Jury at the trial of Selina Stanhope, at the Shire Hall, Nottingham.

BUZZARD, James. School Master and Land Surveyor.

Served on the jury at the inquest into the death of William Stanhope. Resident of Church Street, Market Deeping.

CALTHORP, J G. Coroner at the inquest into the death of William Stanhope, held at the White Horse Inn, Market Deeping.

CHARITY, Samuel. Tailor. Served on the jury at the inquest into the death of William Stanhope. Resident of Stamford Road, Market Deeping.

CHESTERFIELD, Thomas. Farmer of fifty-six acres. Served on the jury at the inquest into the death of William Stanhope. Resident of Market Deeping.

CHURCHMAN, Joseph. Master Tailor. Served on the jury at the inquest into the death of William Stanhope. Resident of High Street, Market Deeping.

CLARK, Police Detective. Supported Police Inspector Thomas Pawson in the questioning and arrest of Selina Stanhope. Stationed in Derby.

CLAYTON, Mary Ann. Gave refuge to Selina Stanhope after leaving Langtoft. Resident of 25 Bridge St, Derby.

CONINGTON, William. Relieving Officer for Bourne Union Workhouse. Resident of Church Street, Market Deeping.

COOK, Joseph. Agricultural Labourer. Gave evidence at initial and resumed inquest into the death of William Stanhope. Resident of High Street, Langtoft.

CROSS, Right Honourable Richard Assheton. Home Secretary. Reprieved Selina Stanhope, 25th November, 1879.

CUCKSON, W T. Served on the Grand Jury at the trial of Selina Stanhope, at the Shire Hall, Nottingham.

DIXON, Elijah. Plumber, Glazier and Painter. Served on the jury at the inquest into the death of William Stanhope. Resident of Church Street, Market Deeping.

DEACON, Elizabeth. Gave evidence at the resumed inquest into the death of William Stanhope. Resident of Church Street, Langtoft.

DEACON, William Beedzler. General Practitioner, Member of Royal College of Surgeons and Licentiate of Apothecaries Society, London. Gave evidence at inquest into the death of William Stanhope. Signed petition for reprieve of Selina Stanhope. Resident of Church Street, Market Deeping.

DEACON, William. Agricultural Labourer. Possibly the father of Selina Stanhope. Resident of Church Street, Langtoft.

DOBNEY, Elizabeth. Stepmother of Selina Stanhope. Gave evidence at the initial and resumed inquest into the death of William Stanhope. Resident of Langtoft.

DOBNEY, Thomas. Stepfather of Selina Stanhope. Resident of Langtoft.

FERRALL, Reverend Charles Whitworth. Vicar of Langtoft. Organised Memorial Petition for the reprieve of Selina Stanhope. Resident of the Rectory, Langtoft.

FFYTCHE, JOHN LEWIS. Served on the Grand Jury at the trial of Selina Stanhope, at the Shire Hall, Nottingham. Resident of Thorpe Hall, South Elkington, Lincolnshire.

FOWLER, Sarah. Wife of Francis Fowler. Agricultural Labourer and Chelsea Pensioner. Gave evidence at the initial and resumed inquest into the death of William Stanhope. Resident of Langtoft.

GILES, John. Master Butcher. Organised memorial petition for the reprieve of Selina Stanhope. Resident of 17 Guildhall Street, Lincoln.

GREEN, Jane Olive. Daughter of Thomas Green, Agricultural Labourer. Gave evidence at the resumed inquest into the death of William Stanhope. Resident of Church Street, behind the Pound, Langtoft.

HARRISON, William. Grocer and Draper. Served on the jury at the inquest into the death of William Stanhope. Resident of Market Place, Market Deeping.

HEYMANN, A. Served on the Grand Jury at the trial of Selina Stanhope, at the Shire Hall, Nottingham.

HOLLAND, James. Farmer of seven hundred and eighty-five acres, employing twenty-one men and eleven boys. Served as Foreman of the Jury at the inquest into the death of William Stanhope. Resident of Elloe, Deeping St Nicholas.

HOLMES, John W. Served on the jury at the trial of Selina Stanhope for the wilful murder of William Stanhope, at the Shire Hall, Nottingham.

HOLMES, William. Farmer of one hundred and fifteen acres, employing two men . Gave evidence at the initial and resumed inquest into the death of William Stanhope. Resident of Farm House, Langtoft.

JACKSON, James. Agricultural Labourer. Gave evidence at the initial and resumed inquest into the death of William Stanhope. Resident of Back Lane, Langtoft.

JEBB, William. Butcher and farmer of twenty-eight acres. Served on the jury at the trial of Selina Stanhope for the wilful murder of William Stanhope at the Shire Hall, Nottingham. Resident of Four Lane Ends, Boughton, Nottinghamshire.

JENNER, Edgar. Master of the Bourne Union Workhouse. Gave evidence at the initial and resumed inquest into the death of Willam Stanhope.

JOHNSON, Samuel. Served on the jury at the trial of Selina Stanhope for the wilful murder of William Stanhope at the Shire Hall, Nottingham.

KENNEDY, Gilbert George, Counsel for the Defence

at the trial of Selina Stanhope, at the Shire Hall, Nottingham. Boarder at the George Hotel, Carlton Street, Nottingham.

KNOWLES, R M. Served on the Grand Jury at the trial of Selina Stanhope, at the Shire Hall, Nottingham.

LIDDELL, Honourable Adolphus Frederick Octavius, Under-Secretary of State for the Home Office, informed Edward Mackay, John Giles and Charles Bradshaw of the Home Secretary's decision to reprieve Selina Stanhope.

LINTON, William. Governor of St John's prison, Nottingham.

LONGFOOT, R. Served on the jury at the inquest into the death of William Stanhope.

LOWE, E J. Served on the Grand Jury at the trial of Selina Stanhope, at the Shire Hall, Nottingham.

MANNERS-SUTTON, J H. Served on the Grand Jury at the trial of Selina Stanhope, at the Shire Hall, Nottingham.

LUMLEY, Edmund. Counsel for the Prosecution at the trial of Selina Stanhope at the Shire Hall, Nottingham.

LUSH, Honourable Robert. Judge at the trial of Selina Stanhope for the wilful murder of William Stanhope, at the Shire Hall, Nottingham.

MACKAY, Major Edward. Governor of Lincoln County prison, Greetwell Road. Received confirmation of the reprieve of Selina Stanhope from the Home Office.

MACONOCHIE, Alexander. Head of the Criminal Department at the Home Office. Coordinated reprieve documents relating to Selina Stanhope.

MATTHEWS, Right Honourable Henry, Home Secretary. Released Selina Stanhope from Woking prison on Conditional Licence.

METHERINGHAM, Joseph. Cottager and shopkeeper. Served on the jury at the trial of Selina Stanhope for the wilful murder of William Stanhope, at the Shire Hall, Nottingham. Resident of Tar Row, Boughton, Nottinghamshire.

NEED, W. Served on the Grand Jury at the trial of Selina Stanhope, at the Shire Hall, Nottingham.

NURSE, Thomas. Farmer of thirty acres. Served on the jury at the inquest into the death of William Stanhope. Resident of Deeping St James.

OXLEY, Joseph. Farmer. Served on the jury at the trial of Selina Stanhope for the wilful murder of William Stanhope at the Shire Hall, Nottingham. Resident of Bole, Nottinghamshire.

PAGET, Joseph. Served on the Grand Jury at the trial of Selina Stanhope, at the Shire Hall, Nottingham.

PARKER, Major William. Justice of the Peace. Committed Selina Stanhope to Lincoln County prison to await trial at the Shire Hall, Nottingham. Resident of Cawthorne House, Bourne.

PAWSON, Thomas. Inspector of Police. Gave evidence at the initial and resumed inquest into the death of

William Stanhope. Resident of the Police Station, Kesteven Division, Market Deeping.

REEDMAN, John. Coal merchant. Resident of Wright's Row, Langtoft.

RICHARDSON, William. Served on the jury at the trial of Selina Stanhope for the wilful murder of William Stanhope at the Shire Hall, Nottingham.

ROBERTSON, Reverend David. Vicar of Market Deeping. Organised memorial petition for the reprieve of Selina Stanhope. Resident of the Rectory, Market Deeping.

SANDERSON, Joseph. Bootmaker employing five men. Served on the jury at the inquest into the death of William Stanhope. Resident of Church Street, Market Deeping.

SAVIDGE, Marshall. Farmer. Served on the jury at the trial of Selina Stanhope for the wilful murder of William Stanhope at the Shire Hall, Nottingham. Resident of Church Square, Gotham, Nottinghamshire.

SEELEY, Charles (Junior). Served on the Grand Jury at the trial of Selina Stanhope, at the Shire Hall, Nottingham.

SHERBROOKE, W. Served on the Grand Jury at the trial of Selina Stanhope, at the Shire Hall, Nottingham.

STANHOPE, Frances. Mother of Selina Stanhope. Married Thomas Dobney. Resident of Langtoft.

STANHOPE, Thomas. Drill man. Grandfather of Selina Stanhope. Resident of Holbeach.

SHILLAKER, William. Baker, employing one man. Served on the jury at the inquest into the death of William Stanhope. Resident of Church Street, Market Deeping.

SMITH, Frederick Chatfield. Head of Smith's Bank, Nottingham and Conservative MP for North Nottinghamshire. Served as Foreman on the Grand Jury at the trial of Selina Stanhope for the murder of William Stanhope, at the Shire Hall, Nottingham. Resident of Bramcote Hall.

STEPHENSON, William Leslie. Grazier and farmer. Served on the jury at the trial of Selina Stanhope for the wilful murder of William Stanhope, at the Shire Hall, Nottingham. Resident of Cedars, Normanton Hill, Normanton upon Soar, Nottinghamshire.

STORER, Charles. Served on the Grand Jury at the trial of Selina Stanhope, at the Shire Hall, Nottingham.

SWIFT, Frederick. Commercial Clerk. Served on the jury at the inquest into the death of William Stanhope. Resident of Church Street, Market Deeping.

TEMPLEMAN, Joseph. Served on the jury at the trial of Selina Stanhope for the wilful murder of William Stanhope, at the Shire Hall, Nottingham.

THACKERAY, J W. Served on the Grand Jury at

the trial of Selina Stanhope, at the Shire Hall, Nottingham.

THORPE, J. Served on the Grand Jury at the trial of Selina Stanhope, at the Shire Hall, Nottingham.

TIDMAS, W. Served on the Grand Jury at the trial of Selina Stanhope, at the Shire Hall, Nottingham.

WARRAND, W. Served on the Grand Jury at the trial of Selina Stanhope, at the Shire Hall, Nottingham.

WEBB, W F. Served on the Grand Jury at the trial of Selina Stanhope, at the Shire Hall, Nottingham.

WILMSHURST, Edwin. Ironmonger. Served on the jury at the trial of Selina Stanhope for the wilful murder of William Stanhope, at the Shire Hall, Nottingham. Resident of 7 Market Square, East Retford, Nottinghamshire.

WOOD, James. Served on the jury at the trial of Selina Stanhope for the wilful murder of William Stanhope at the Shire Hall, Nottingham.

WOOD, William. Served on the jury at the trial of Selina Stanhope for the wilful murder of William Stanhope at the Shire Hall, Nottingham.

Appendix Two

Summary Catalogue of the Contents of Home Office File 144/50/88782

The descriptions below record the contents of the Home Office file relating to the reprieve of Selina Stanhope in 1879 and only made accessible to the public in 1990.

Editorial note: in the early stages of the process, the documents in the file passed through the hands of mainly anonymous Home Office clerks, who signalled their part in the process with a squiggled initial: these have been noted even though sometimes indecipherable. Some words have been abbreviated by the person dealing with the document when writing brief minutes, which I have expanded within brackets; words which were impossible to read I have signalled by a blank space within brackets.

Letter, memorial and petition from the Rev C W Ferrall, dated 17ᵗʰ November, 1879

Home Office Notes and Annotations
- Stamped 18ᵗʰ November, 1879, Department 1
- Numbered: 88782/1
- Titled: Selina Stanhope, Lincoln Assizes?, November 1879, Murder, Death.
- Docketed: The Reverend C W Ferrale (*sic*) forwards Memorial, signed by himself, Churchwardens and Parishioners of Langtoft, Lincs, praying that S[ecretary] of S[tate] will represent to Her Majesty the desirability of extending Her Royal Clemency to the above, and commute the sentence, passed on her, to a lesser punishment. Believe that desperation of her state led her to commit the crime.
- Notes: Pressing; Mr Justice Lush (beneath docket); initialled SO; Ack[nowledge]d; initialled Alexander Maconochie; Wrote to M J Lush 18.11.79; Inf[ormed] of respite

25.11.79; to Judge for Notes and Reports; initialled Alexander Maconochie; 18.11.79.

Letter from Murray Finch-Hatton, High Sheriff of Lincolnshire, Haverholme Priory, dated 18th November, 1879, addressed to Augustus Liddell

Home Office Notes and Annotations
- Stamped: 18th November, 1879, Department 1
- Numbered: 88782/2
- Titled: Selina Stanhope. Lincoln Prison.
- Docketed: High Sheriff of Lincolnshire states that 9 a.m. on Monday, December 1st, has been fixed for the execution of the above. Adds that the address, Haverholme Priory, Sleaford – will find him, if required, to communicate with him any further on the subject.
- Notes: Pressing

Letter from Robert Lush, relating to trial notes and report, dated 18th November, 1879

Home Office Notes and Annotations
- Stamped: 19th November, 1879, Department 1
- Numbered: 88782/3
- Titled: Selina Stanhope
- Docketed: Mr Justice Lush forwards a copy of his notes with recommendation to mercy,

and reports on the case. See further letter to
S[ecretary] of S[tate] within.

- Notes: Pressing; I think effect might be given
in this case to the recommendation of the
jury and the sentence be commuted to p[enal]
s[ervitude] for life. It is in all [ ] with the [ ]
and other similar cases and presents the usual
grounds for commutation. In new hand: I will
see the judge next week. Arrange for Monday
or Tuesday; dated 20/11/79 and initialled
Richard Assheton Cross; in another hand:
I have written to the judge; dated 24/11/79,
initialled [ ]

Letter from Mr John Giles, forwarding a petition signed by citizens of Lincoln, undated

Home Office Notes and Annotations
- Stamped: 24th November, 1879, Department 1
- Numbered: 88782/4
- Docketed: Mr John Giles forwards a petition
from the inhabitants of Lincoln praying that
the sentence of death passed on the above
may not be carried out.
- Notes: Pressing; inf[orme]d of respite 25.11.79

Letter from the minister, churchwardens and parishioners of Market Deeping petitioning the commutation of the death penalty, undated

Home Office Notes and Annotations
- Stamped: none
- Numbered: 88782/4
- Titled: none
- Docketed: none
- Notes: Reply

Memorial petition from Thomas John Nathaniel Brogden, the Mayor of Lincoln, undated

Home Office Notes and Annotations
- Stamped: 24th November, 1879, Department 1
- Numbered: 88782/5
- Titled: Selina Stanhope
- Docketed: Mayor of Lincoln and others resident in the County pray for commutation of sentence of above on the ground that the crime was committed when prisoner was in a state of nearly approaching madness, urge also the recommendation to mercy by the jury.
- Notes: Pressing; initialled JO; Ack[nowledge]d 24/11/79; The judge says the jury was an excellent one. I would advise giving consideration to

their very strong recommendation. The young woman was driven to desperation; 24/11/79; initialled Alexander Maconochie; Respite and commutation to P[enal] S[ervitude] for Life; Inf[ormed] of respite 25.11.79

Letter from Mr William James Towner, proprietor of the *Brighton Gazette*, requesting mercy for Selina Stanhope, dated 23rd November, 1879

Home Office Notes and Annotations
- Stamped: 24th November, 1879, Department 1
- Numbered: 88782/6
- Titled: Selina Stanhope
- Docketed: Mr W[illiam] Towner prays for S[ecretary] of S[tate]'s merciful consid[eratio]n of the sentence of death passed on the above. Forwards a newspaper extract commenting upon the case.
- Notes: Inf[orme]d of respite. 25.11.79

Letter from Charles Bradshaw, Acting Under-Sheriff, Nottingham, petitioning the commutation of the death sentence of Selina Stanhope, on behalf of the jurors, dated 25th November, 1879

Home Office Notes and Annotations

- Stamped: 26[th] November, 1879, Department 1
- Numbered: 88782/7
- Titled: Selina Stanhope
- Docketed: Acting Under-Sheriff of Nottingham forwards a petition from the jurors who tried the case praying for the commutation of the sentence of the above on the grounds of the circumstances under which the crime was committed.
- Notes: Pressing; Inform him of Respite; initialled Alexander Maconochie; SO wrote 26.11.79

Telegraph letter from Edward Mackay, Governor of Lincoln Prison, dated 26th November, 1879, acknowledging receipt of respite of Selina Stanhope

Home Office Notes and Annotations
- Stamped: 26[th] November, 1879, Department 1
- Numbered: 88782/8
- Titled: Selina Stanhope
- Docketed: Governor of Lincoln Prison acknowledges by telegraph letter respiting execution of death passed on above
- Notes: Pressing; [   ] initialled by Alexander Maconochie; Cond[itiona]l Pardon; 27.11.79

Telegraph letter from Alfred Burton, acting Under-Sheriff for Lincolnshire, dated 26th November, 1879

Home Office Notes and Annotations
- Stamped: 26th November, 1879, Department 1
- Numbered: 88782/9
- Titled: Selina Stanhope
- Docketed: Acting Under-Sheriff of Lincolnshire acknowledges by telegraph, receipt of respite in this case
- Notes: Pressing; [   ]; initialled by Alexander Maconochie

Letter from William James Towner expressing gratitude to Home Secretary for reprieve of Selina Stanhope, dated 26th November, 1879

Home Office Notes and Annotations
- Numbered: 88782/10

Letter from Edward Mackay, Governor of Lincoln Prison, dated 26th November, 1879, acknowledging receipt of respite of Selina Stanhope

Home Office Notes and Annotations
- Stamped: 27th November, 1879
- Numbered: 88782/10

- Titled: Selina Stanhope
- Docketed: The Governor of HM Prison, Lincoln, ack[nowledgement] of H[ome] O[ffice] letter of 25 inst., conveying the Queen's commands that the execution of the sentence of death be respited;
- Notes: [   ]; initialled Alexander Maconochie

Telegraph letter from Edward Mackay, Governor of Lincoln Prison, dated 27th November, 1879, acknowledging receipt of respite of Selina Stanhope

Home Office Notes and Annotations
- Stamped: 27th November, 1879
- Numbered: 88782/11
- Titled: Selina Stanhope. Lincoln Prison.
- Docketed: Governor acknowledges by telegram receipt of the respite of the execution of the sentence of death passed on the above
- Notes: [   ]; initialled Alexander Maconochie

Letter from Alfred Burton, acting Under-Sheriff for Lincolnshire, dated 26th November, 1879, acknowledging receipt of respite of Selina Stanhope

Home Office Notes and Annotations
- Stamped: 27th November, 1879

- Numbered: 88782/12
- Titled: Selina Stanhope. Lincoln Prison.
- Docketed: Acting Under-Sheriff for the County of Lincoln, acknowledges receipt of H<ome> O[ffice] letter of 25 inst., relative to the respite of the execution of the sentence passed on the above
- Notes: [   ]; initialled Alexander Maconochie

Telegraph letter from Edward Mackay, Governor of Lincoln Prison, dated 27th November, 1879, acknowledging receipt of a duplicate letter related to respite of Selina Stanhope

Home Office Notes and Annotations
- Stamped: 28th November, 1879
- Numbered: 88782/13
- Titled: Selina Stanhope
- Docketed: Lincoln Governor acknowledges receipt of H[ome] O[ffice]'s letter of 25 inst., informing him that the sentence passed on above has been respited
- Notes: [   ]; initialled Alexander Maconochie

Miscellaneous administrative documents relating to early release from Woking prison, including a petition from the prison chaplain and another, probably written by Selina Stanhope herself;

official reports from Woking prison on her behaviour; a copy of the Conditional Licence granted by the Home Secretary; and a letter recording the exchange from a Conditional <u>Licence to an Ordinary Licence.</u>

Home Office Notes and Annotations
- Stamped: 9th July, 1887 – 4th December, 1889
- Numbered: 88782/15, 88782/16, 88782/17a, 88782/18, 88782/19

Appendix Three

Transcriptions of Key Documents in the Reprieve of Selina Stanhope

Document: 88782/3 (part)
Letter from Robert Lush, relating to trial notes and report, dated 18th November, 1879
(3 pages)

> *60 Avenue Road, Nov. 18, 1879*
>
> *Dear Mr Cross*
> *I had first made up this report ready for the first post in the morning when your letter was delivered.*

I was much pressed at Warwick when I finished last night, but as only the Sunday had passed I / felt that there was plenty of time. I do not know that I can say more than I have said. I should be happy to call on any day at the closing of the Commons should you ask to see me.

I enclose the petitions. / The other case you shall have in a day or two.

Robert Lush

The woman is no doubt by this time in the Gaol at Lincoln.

Document:88782/3 (part)

Letter from Robert Lush, containing trial notes, dated 18th November, 1879

(6 pages)

60 Avenue Road, Nov. 18, 1879

Selina Stanhope

Sir

This woman was tried before me at Nottingham yesterday week, the 10th inst. for the murder of her illegitimate child – a boy of between 8 and 9 months old – and found guilty, the Jury adding a strong recommendation to mercy./

She is a woman I think of about 23 or 24 years of age, but I omitted to note the age in my book, and I cannot recollect precisely the age accredited to her in the Calendar. She was a domestic servant

apparently of a very low type, although described
by one of the witnesses as of an average strength of
mind – Edgar Jennings p.3.

There is no doubt about the facts or the propriety
of the / verdict.

She went in the early part of June to the house of
her stepfather, having with her the child. The father
was ill and unable to work and his second wife
laboured in the fields. They were very poor, and the
girl was not a welcome guest. Indeed the stepfather
said he could not do with her.

On the 26ᵗʰ June she was admitted into the
Workhouse as a destitute pauper & remained there
til the 17ᵗʰ July. She then left of her own accord
& went back to / her stepfather. On the following
evening she left with the child without saying where
she was going, and, after about 2 hours returned
without the child stating that she put it out where it
would be well taken care of. In the interval she was
observed sitting by the road side near a small stream
or channel, apparently nursing the child. She took
away her box the same night to a Carrier's & early
the next morning left, having told a neighbour she
was going to Derby. She never returned. /

Three days afterwards the body of the child was
found lying in another channel, a short distance from
the one where she was first seen, having been in the
water apparently some days. It was entirely naked

& the clothes it wore when she left her step father's house were found in her box at Derby when she was apprehended. Death was caused by drowning. There was no mark of violence on the / body.

I enclose a copy of my notes with the recommendation to mercy. I did not ask the grounds of the recommendation. It was obviously based on sympathy for the girl and I think repugnance to capital punishment in the case of an infant.

I am sir, your obedient servant,
Robert Lush

Document: 88782/4

Letter from Mr John Giles, forwarding a petition signed by citizens of Lincoln, undated
(3 pages)

17 Guildhall St, Lincoln
To the Home Secretary
The Right Honourable R. A. Cross

The inhabitants of the City of Lincoln feeling desirous to give expression to their feelings regarding the unhappy Girl, Selina Stanhope, who was sentenced to Death at the Nottingham Assizes for Child Murder have ventured to approach you by Petition to solicit the Clemency of the Crown, praying the Sentence / of the Law may be mercifully withdrawn, and that such punishment may be awarded as you feel fit after a consideration of all the Circumstances of the Case.

The Petition forwarded to you Comprises the most influential of our City and could be augmented by thousands, but as the Mayor, Sheriff, Justices of the Peace and Corporators who have had an opportunity have forwarded to you their / names we feel sure it will fully impress you with the anxiety of your Petitioners on her behalf. Our City Members, C Seely Esq and Colonel Chaplin being absent from London are very sorry the petition cannot have their support and presentation and beg respectfully to be pardoned thus anticipating upon your Consideration.

Yours most obediently and Respectfully
John Giles

Document: 88782/5

Letter from the rector, churchwardens and parishioners of Market Deeping petitioning the commutation of the death penalty, undated

To the Right Honourable R A Cross, Her Majesty's
Secretary of State for the Home Department.
Sir,

We the undersigned the Minister, Churchwardens and parishioners of the parish of Market Deeping, Lincolnshire, desire to bring under your notice the

case of Selina Stanhope, now lying under sentence of death for the crime of infanticide lately committed in the parish of Langtoft, Lincolnshire, & trust that Her Majesty may be induced to commute the said penalty by such lesser punishment as may seem fitting. We believe the circumstances of her case have been made known to you & we hope that you will so represent the matter to Her Majesty that she may be pleased to extend Her Royal Mercy to the said Selina Stanhope.

> *We remain,*
> *Sir, Your obedient Servants*
> *David Robertson, Rector*

Document 88782/5

Memorial petition from Thomas John Nathaniel Brogden, the Mayor of Lincoln, undated
(2 pages)

> *To the Right Honourable the Secretary of State for the Home Office*
>
> *The Memorial of us the undersigned residents of the County of Lincoln humbly Sheweth.*

1. *That your memorialists beg your especial attention to the case of Selina Stanhope who was sentenced to death for the murder of her illegitimate child at Langtoft at the recent assizes held at Nottingham for the County of Lincoln.*

2. *That your memorialists are of opinion that*

all the circumstances attending the murder should be well weighed and considered before the extreme penalty of the Law is allowed to be carried into effect in this instance.

3. *That your memorialists are supported in their opinion by the evidence adduced at the trial from which it appeared that the mother was totally uneducated and although reared in the greatest poverty and apparently amid surroundings of the lowest moral type and development yet was truly fond of her child and had hitherto tended it with all the care at her command. These circumstances suggest that she must have committed the act which brought about her child's death while in a state nearly approaching madness, caused by misery and depression consequent perhaps on the feeling that she herself was fatherless and motherless and without a home in which to leave her babe while she again went out into the world to earn a livelihood.*

4. *That your memorialists are further supported in this opinion by the recommendation to mercy of the Jury / who tried the prisoner.*

Your memorialists therefore humbly pray that you may see fit to commute the sentence of death passed on the said Selina Stanhope.

And your memorialists will ever pray et cetera.

Document 88782/6

Letter from Mr William James Towner, proprietor of the *Brighton Gazette*, requesting mercy for Selina Stanhope, dated 23rd November, 1879

Brighton Gazette
Curtis Bros & Towner, Proprietors
Offices: 150, North Street, Brighton
111a, Western Road, Hove

November 23rd/79

Right Hon. & dear Sir

    I crave your pardon for approaching you, but having read the accompanying article in the News of the World of the above date & feeling that it has been dictated by the divinest powers the writer possesses, I implore you read it – it will strengthen you with the desire & I pray encourage you to grant mercy to the wretched unfortunate Selina Stanhope. God will be on your side, dear Sir, as His mercy will follow yours & Our Saviour's blessing accompany you for her salvation from the gallows. That the guidance of the Holy Spirit will be yours in this distressing case is the sincere prayer of

    Your most obedient Servant
    William J Towner

(In margin: I know that your enormous duties

prevent recognition of all correspondences but I shall
be happy to know that my poor plea reached you.)

Document 88782/15

H M Prison Pro Forma Petition from the Acting
Chaplin of Woking Prison to Henry Matthews, Home
Secretary, on behalf of Selina Stanhope, dated 7th July,
1887, requesting her early release

Date: *7th July, 1887*
Register Number: *F147*
Name: *Selina Stanhope*
Present Age: *32 years*
Confined in: *Woking Female Convict Prison*
Convicted when: *6th November, 1879*
Convicted where: *Nottingham Assizes*
Crime: *Wilful Murder*
Sentence: *Life P[enal] S[ervitude]*
Remarks: *Conduct fair* (signed W Clarke)

To the Right Honourable Henry Matthews Her
Majesty's Principal Secretary of State for the Home
Department.
The Petition of Selina Stanhope, a prisoner in the
above named prison.
HUMBLY SHEWETH –

That your Petitioner humbly begs you will take her

case into your kind and merciful consideration. She is sentenced to Penal Servitude for life, and is now in the eighth year of her sentence. She most humbly pleads that a favourable veiw (sic) may be taken of her case, and her liberty granted her, when she will endeavour to prove by future life, that she is sincerely repentant for the past. Your Petitioner has all through her imprisonment been in correspondence with respectable friends, who would gladly receive her from prison, and help her to lead an honourable life in the future. And your Petitioner as in duty bound will ever pray etc etc.

Your Humble Petitioner

(In margin for official notes only: *Prays for remission of life sentence; Pleads good intentions for the future and help of friends; J Cat [   ] acting Chaplin*)

Document 88782/15

H M Prison Pro Forma Petition from Woking prison to Henry Matthews, Home Secretary, on behalf of Selina Stanhope, dated 12th February, 1889, requesting her early release

<u>Date</u>: *12 February, 1889*
<u>Register Number</u>: *F147*
<u>Name</u>: *Selina Stanhope*
<u>Present Age</u>: *33 years*

Confined in: *Woking Female Convict Prison*
Convicted when: *6th November, 1879*
Convicted where: *Nottingham Assizes*
Crime: *Murder*
Sentence: *Life Penal Serv[itude]*
Remarks: *Conduct good* (signed M Hutchinson)

*To the Right Honourable Her Majesty's Principal
Secretary of State for the Home Department.
The Petition of the above named prisoner
HUMBLY SHEWETH –*

*Your humble petitioner prays for a merceful (sic)
consideratione (sic) of her very unhappy case a life
sentence she has now completed more than nine long
weary years she pleade (sic) for mercy she feels her
degraded position mosst (sic) deeply she in her hours
of loneliness dwelling on her case wondering how
she could have commetted (sic) such a fearful crime
[   ] must have for [   ] her for the time for she
love her Boy most dearly and at this moment would
sacrifice her own life to bring him back she pleads in
extenuatione (sic) of her crime she knows she is only
suffering the due penalty of the law should mercy be
granted her she long to prove gratitude by her future
life she has very respectable friends willing to receive
her she should humble (sic) pray the Secretary of
State to look with mercy and pity on her case.*

S Stanhope

Postscript

The Reprieve Examined

The newspaper reports on the reprieve of Selina Stanhope made it clear that there was considerable concern in the county that a young woman who had endured such a pitifully unhappy life was now facing the extreme penalty of the law.

The memorials received by the Home Office from Lincoln, Nottingham and Langtoft, were in agreement with the jury that whilst Selina Stanhope was guilty of committing an appalling crime, the circumstances of her life were strong arguments against her execution. The common themes of isolation, brutal rejection and poverty leading to an anguished act of desperation – what the Nottingham memorial termed 'a sudden frenzy'- ran through all three documents as unarguable reasons for sparing her life. In addition, such social misfortune had been exacerbated by the ethical deficiencies of not having had 'proper early training', according to the Langtoft memorial, and having had to live 'amid surroundings of the lowest moral type', according to the Lincoln memorial. All three were clear that Selina Stanhope did not kill her child with malice aforethought, but had acted in a state of extreme misery and depression resulting from her quite miserable circumstances.

The emotive and rational arguments for a reprieve would no doubt have carried some weight in the final reckoning by the Home Office. However, the social composition of the petitioners as much as such familiar arguments, may have made a greater impact, assuming that the document was given more than a cursory inspection by the decision makers.

The Lincoln petition, as noted by John Giles in his letter, was signed by many of the city's most distinguished citizens, in addition to being explicitly endorsed by Lincoln's two Members of Parliament. Mr Giles suggested in his letter that the petition could be 'augmented by thousands' which may have been more of a fanciful rhetorical claim than a factually accurate one. The memorial petition received by the Home Office from Lincoln consisted of twenty-six names, many of whom had also supported the reprieve of Emma Wade.

The Nottingham petition, which in fact arrived the day after the Home Secretary had granted a respite from execution, consisted of the entire jury and perhaps most interestingly, the Counsel for the Prosecution. Had it arrived on time, it may well have made a telling contribution to the reprieve of Selina Stanhope, although in view of the fact that the petition was signed by the jury which had recommended mercy in the first place, its impact may not have been decisive.

The most interesting memorial petitions were from Langtoft and from nearby Market Deeping. Both documents were put together by local clerics on flimsy sheets of paper which have suffered greater wear and tear than the more formally presented memorial petition from Lincoln. However, the sense of hurried informality in the Langtoft document, containing eighty-four signatures, and in the Market Deeping petition containing twelve names, creates a greater sense of concerned communal urgency. Significantly, the petition from Langtoft was the first document to be received at Whitehall, on 18th November.

Unsurprisingly, both petitions contain the names of respected professional men, such as the William Deacon who performed the post mortem on William Stanhope, as well as distinguished members of the local farming community, such as the Peasgood family. The extensively signed Langtoft document, however, indicates a significant degree of support and sympathy from less privileged backgrounds, such as agricultural labourers James Christian and Thomas Coddington, both resident in humble cottages on the High Street. It also included the names of men and women who were at the centre of everyday village life, such as William and Kate Seth who ran the Royal Oak public house on Bourne Road and Thomas Wakeling who with his wife, Jane Wakeling, ran the village baker and grocer's shop.

Letters of support for Emma Wade received by the Home Office from beyond the county of Lincolnshire reflected the wider interest in the case generated by the popular press. Conversely, the relative lack of serious media interest in Selina Stanhope is indicated by there being only one document in the Home Office file from outside of the county, from Mr William James Towner, one of the proprietors of the *Brighton Gazette* newspaper, accompanied by a clipping taken from *The News of the World*, published on Sunday, 23rd November, 1879.

The clipping was a lengthy letter to the editor, filling two columns of dense print, which drew attention to the plight of Selina Stanhope, arguing that it 'brought into light the cruelty of the law, which should be guided by an intelligent and unerring principle of justice'. It was an interesting letter in many respects, both in terms of its concerns and the language used to express them.

The correspondent, who pseudonymously signed himself as Hampden, was clearly very familiar with the case. He outlined in great detail the established facts about the misfortunes of Selina Stanhope whilst embroidering them with a few speculative fictions of his own. In addition, it is obvious that he was using the troubles of Selina Stanhope to support his outraged polemic against the bastardy laws as they had evolved piecemeal in the nineteenth-century and their catastrophic consequences for women like Selina Stanhope.

His opening broadside was aimed at men who seduced women, typically domestic servants, leaving them alone to endure shame and poverty: 'The ruin of a girl entails neither penalty nor discomfort to her betrayer', he insisted. The inadequacy of the law permits a man to escape responsibility for his actions when both common justice and common humanity suggest that the father of an infant should be compelled to pay for its maintenance, rather than leaving the mother to bear the burden alone. The writer is genuinely sympathetic to any woman in the distressed situation he describes, although, in passing, he does make reference to the cost to the ratepayer of supporting the destitute in the workhouse.

There is a sense that the writer, at this point, was

finding it difficult to restrain himself and remain within the constraints of reasoned argument. What followed in its sensationalism and melodramatic pathos was the stuff of unbridled reformist zeal. How is a poor girl to live, he demands to know, 'with not a friend in the world, unable to hide her disgrace, and turned from by other girls and women?' On this point, the law does not pretend to have an opinion, although it does require such a girl to support her child. To its shame, what the law does allow is that 'she may lie down in the street with her child at her breast and die there'.

There is also a strong sense of empathy with the people of Langtoft caught up in a difficult and, at times, impossible situation. The condition of the father, 'laid up and disabled from earning a shilling' when his stepdaughter returned home was as pitiable as his vexed reaction was understandable. The generosity and care shown towards Selina Stanhope by the 'kind-hearted' Elizabeth Fowler was recognised as a good deed in a wicked world, although his tentative proposal that the carter who had thoughtfully offered her a lift 'may have suggested to her distracted mind a happy home, and a wife also with a baby at her breast, to whom life was a pleasure', was perhaps a sentiment too far.

The final quarter of the letter was an articulate and reasoned attack on the 'inconsiderate law put upon

the statute book by Lord Brougham some thirty or
forty years ago', but before that the writer used the sad
case of Selina Stanhope in one final attempt to engage
the sympathies of the reader on an emotional level,
and in so doing perhaps fell into the trap awaiting all
passionate exponents of justice and reform. The care
and affection shown by the mother towards her child
were recognised in court and were strong arguments
on a rational level for reprieve. However, the writer
was not content with recording strong mitigating
circumstances in a sad case of the drowning of a small
child, which he thought any Home Secretary would
find hard to resist. Instead, drawing upon the worst
excesses of self-indulgent and maudlin Victorian
poetry, he invented a scene which supposedly took
place at the side of the drain and which unashamedly
pushed sentimental hyperbole to its limit:

> 'The outcast, homeless, hopeless, destitute,
> despairing girl hung over her babe, closely pressing
> it with all a mother's fondness of heart; the sun was
> shining in the blue heaven, birds sang around her,
> the brooklet murmured softly at her feet; all seemed
> to speak of comfort, harmony and peace; things lost
> to her for ever.'

After having analysed the shortcomings of Lord
Brougham's legislation which essentially let the

putative father of an illegitimate child off the hook, the writer ended his letter on the subject of acquittals on the grounds of temporary insanity. It was a highly contentious issue which the writer thought had a pressing relevance to the case of a destitute girl 'driven to despair and madness', after having been abandoned by her 'professed lover, the father of the child'. More broadly, such temporary insanity was a significant factor in the increasing number of cases of infanticide which should alert the country's legislators to an urgent reform of the law.

It was a calm ending to a sometimes turbulent letter.

The words of 'Hampden' had clearly moved William Towner to write in support of Selina Stanhope's reprieve, describing them admiringly as having been 'dictated by the divinest powers the writer possesses'. The letter from Mr Towner was also clearly prompted by his personal faith, assuring the Home Secretary that God would be on his side should he grant Selina Stanhope 'salvation from the gallows'. He also reassured Richard Cross of his prayers that the guidance of the Holy Spirit would be given to him in dealing with the difficulties of such a distressing case.

Willam Towner was both fervent and sincere, if a little quirky, and was even moved to write a second letter on 26th November thanking the Home Secretary for his 'merciful sympathy'; but perhaps, like John Bright in his concern for Emma Wade, the sending of a sympathetic clipping from a well-known London newspaper may possibly have sufficed.

The most extensive document in the Home Office file related to the reprieve of Selina Stanhope is the set of notes written by Justice Lush during the course of the trial, consisting of twenty-one pages in total. Alongside his post-trial reflections on the case, the notes would have carried the greatest written weight for a Home Secretary and his advisors in reaching a decision. The notes had the authority of the judge's legal status as a professional adjudicator of what evidence heard in court was most relevant to an understanding of the case, whilst his social status and reputation would have been a reassuring guarantee of both reliability and accuracy.

In the final analysis, however, such trial notes are just one narrative, written down in the form of loosely constructed observations, which should be placed alongside other narratives of the trial which were published in the newspapers. The accounts found in the *Lincolnshire Chronicle*, the *Stamford Mercury* and the notebook of Justice Lush are all three a product of selection for a purpose and a particular audience, and so whilst constructing a narrative from the same material, they inevitably produced variants and variations in content and emphasis.

The trial notes of Justice Lush record the evidence of the various witnesses and in broad terms are a duplication of the accounts constructed in the media. However, they also include details of the process which were either not mentioned by the court reporters or were briefly skirted over, some of which provide a greater clarity on the court proceedings, especially on the closing remarks made by the Counsel for the Defence.

The notes relating to the deposition of Edgar Jenner, the Master of the Bourne Union Workhouse, focused upon the administrative facts of Selina Stanhope's reception into the workhouse and her exemplary behaviour during her short stay. They also emphasise how kindly the infant was treated by its mother and how healthy it appeared to Mr Jenner. According to the final comment, 'Her mind was all right – a strong mind I should say – average'. The report of Jenner's evidence, evinced under cross-examination, which was reported in the *Lincolnshire Chronicle,* also records his judgement about the state of mind of Selina Stanhope: as far as he knew, her mind was 'not affected in any way'. The two versions of Jenner's words, possibly trying to convey the same idea that Selina Stanhope did not show any signs of problems with her mental health, are slightly different in their nuance: the newspaper version is a generalised statement of mental wellbeing, whilst that recorded by Justice Lush, apparently a verbatim quotation from Jenner, seems to suggest a determination of character, as much as a balance of mind. The exact meaning of Edwin Jenner's observation is further complicated by a third version of his words, found in Justice Lush's post-trial report, in which he seems to re-hash the words of the witness and in the process alter their meaning: 'She was a domestic servant apparently of a very low type, although described by one of the witnesses as of an average strength of mind – Edgar Jennings p.3'.

Robert Lush's most extensive notes were given over to the deposition of Elizabeth Dobney, whose involvement in the downward spiral of her step-daughter's life was various: she had grudgingly lived with her, she did not conceal her dislike of her and she gave hostile evidence against her at the inquest in Market Deeping concerning her attitude towards the child, as well as herself.

Mrs Dobney appeared to be a great observer of any human inadequacy, except her own.

The six pages of deposition given over to the testimony of Elizabeth Dobney, some of which was already in the public domain, reinforces the image of her as a passive bystander, who most of the time either claimed not no know what had happened or chose not to be involved in what was happening. To some extent, this was evident from the media reports of her words at Market Deeping and at the Nottingham Assizes. The trial notes of Robert Lush which record material not mentioned in the newspaper reports, however, create a stronger sense of a woman either unable or unwilling to support Selina Stanhope; even worse, that she was in complete denial concerning any kind of responsibility for the unfolding events in Langtoft between June and July, 1879.

Justice Lush noted her assertion that Selina Stanhope had not been confined at her house and that she had turned up unexpectedly with an infant child about a fortnight before she entered the workhouse. They also record her insistence that 'she left us of her own account'.

What is most striking about the distillation of the deposition by the judge is the number of statements which declared what she didn't know. When Selina Stanhope left the house to go to the workhouse in Bourne, 'She did not say where she was going or why she went'. When told that the infant had been left in the care of a nurse, 'she did not say at whose house, and I did not ask more'. After returning to the house without the child, she went upstairs, but Mrs Dobney 'did not see her come in'. She had returned to collect her box from upstairs and take it to Mr Reedman's house: Mrs Dobney had seen her bring the box downstairs and put it in a barrow, but 'could not see what was in it'. On her return to the house, late in the evening, her stepdaughter had tea, but Elizabath Dobney 'asked no questions.'

After having shared a bed with Mrs Dobney's ten year-old daughter for the night, Selina Stanhope came downstairs between 7 and 8 o'clock, but she couldn't say 'whether she had breakfast'. On departing the house for the final time, she 'didn't say where she was going or whether she was coming back'.

Under cross-examination, Mrs Dobney's memory continued to remain stubbornly deficient, it seems. On being pressed about the whereabouts of Selina Stanhope before her return to Langtoft, she replied, 'I can't say where she had been living before she came with the child'. On her return from the workhouse, 'She did not hear [her] husband say anything to her'. On the morning of the alleged murder, she could not remember if Selina Stanhope was wearing 'any cloak or shawl' nor could she recall what dress she was wearing, although she did remember that she was dressed in black when she left for the house for the final time: it was a useful recollection. The lack of clarity about the clothes was in sharp contrast with her instant recognition in court of the clothes worn by William Stanhope on the day of his death, even down to a small pair of striped socks. 'These are they', she had stated without hesitation, according to the judge's notes.

Many of the denials and evasions of Elizabeth Dobney were reported in the press, but in the compressed context of Justice Lush's brief notes, which also included hitherto unrecorded material of a similar nature, it strongly reinforced a sense of dysfunctionality, personal antipathies or both.

The notes of the judge also confirmed the *Lincolnshire Chronicle* report that Mrs Dobney passed by the drain when William Stanhope's naked body was being pulled out the water. Similarly, they did not record any conversation having taken place during the course of such an extraordinary incident: 'Saw the Police Inspector taking the body of a child out of the water – it was Prisoner's', was all she told the court.

The various reports related to the three land workers who had encountered Selina Stanhope near the bridge presented some difficulties in terms of consistency. The *Stamford Mercury*'s report on the resumed inquest identified the witnesses as James Jackson, Joseph Cook and Henry Bell. The *Grantham Journal* identified the same three men, but foregrounded Joseph Cook, rather than James Jackson as the key player in the incident. Whilst the report of the trial in the *Lincolnshire Chronicle* also highlighted the importance of the deposition of Joseph Cook, rather than James Jackson, it also the identified the third land worker on his way home as Henry Dobney.

The notes of Justice Lush to some extent resolve the inconsistencies, but at the same time generate new ones.

His notes record a substantial deposition by Joseph Cook, whilst James Jackson was reduced to a passing mention by Cook. The introduction of Henry Dobney in the *Lincolnshire Chronicle* does not seem to have been a mistake by the reporter, in that Justice Lush mentioned Cook saying, 'I was driving home from Market Deeping in a cart. Jackson and one Dawbney (*sic*) in the cart with me'. Henry Dobney, like Henry Bell whom he replaced, seems to have been a silent witness. The reason for the disappearance of Henry Bell from the narrative and the arrival of Henry Dobney is impossible to explain. However, it is a curious fact that an agricultural labourer by the name of William Henry Dobney, aged sixteen, is recorded in the Census of 1871 as living with his grandfather, Henry Bell, also an agricultural labourer in Langtoft.

The notes assembled from Joseph Cook's deposition tend to focus upon local information related to distances between Langtoft and Market Deeping, the precise location of bridges and drains separating the parish boundaries and the time of arrival at the bridge. The offer of a lift and Selina Stanhope's refusal were recorded by Justice Lush, as they were in the newspaper, but the main point of interest seemed to be her sitting on the grass slope with her feet towards the nearby drain, her back towards him and her leaning over something. Besides telling the court that he did not notice her dress, under cross-examination Mr Cook also said that he was only about two yards away from her and that the dyke was around five feet wide.

The evidence of Olive Green was heard both at the inquest and at the trial: a comparison between the two depositions, as reported by the press, highlights some inconsistency of detail, in particular, as to whether she had actually seen the baby in his mother's arms at the bridge or had just heard him cry. On both occasions, she had also provided telling evidence against Selina Stanhope, deposing that she had noticed her dress being wet when she saw her late in the evening, and further, she had later overheard the subject being discussed by Elizabeth Deacon and Selina Stanhope. Her evidence at the inquest gave precise details of the conversation between Selina Stanhope and Elizabeth Deacon, but these were not repeated at the trial: she had observed a conversation, it seems, but no more. The trial notes of the judge explicitly confirm that Olive Green only saw a conversation and that she did not hear a single word of it: 'Elizabeth Deacon was standing about ten yards from me. They spoke, I did not hear what was said'. It may be that Olive Green, like some other witnesses, found it difficult to distinguish between what she thought she saw and heard at the time and what she had later been told had happened.

According to the notebook, Olive Green, in words very similar to those of Joseph Cook, described Selina Stanhope 'sitting on the grass – close to the Bridge – her feet towards Dyke'. In addition to the account found in the *Lincolnshire Chronicle*, under cross-examination, Olive Green said that Selina Stanhope was wearing a light print dress at the bridge and further, that there was 'something dark over her dress, but she did not notice what'. Possibly in an attempt by the Defence to undermine the significance of the evidence concerning the wet dress, it seems that Olive Green was asked about whether the dress was wet at the front as well as at the back: according to Justice Lush's notes, she 'did not notice her dress was wet in front'.

What was clear in Olive Green's memory was that when she saw Selina Stanhope return to the village from the bridge she was carrying 'a fancy basket, nothing else': it was an interesting, if irrelevant adjective. The report of the trial by the *Stamford Mercury* clearly thought that her entire testimony was irrelevant to a full understanding of the case, as it is was completely omitted.

Three pages of Robert Lush's notes are given over to the deposition of Sarah Fowler whose account of events at the inquest and the trial, as reported, were consistent and coherent. Possibly the only note of additional interest related to the giving of bread and butter to a distressed Selina Stanhope on the second visit to see Sarah Fowler, accompanied by her young brother. In both the inquest and the trial reports, the young woman had been unable to eat the bread and butter; according to the judge's notes, however, Sarah Fowler had told the court that Selina had declined the food, but had given it to her young brother. It was an act of kindness which contrasted with the rather unforgiving image created by her stepmother.

The notes taken from the deposition of William Holmes, the no-nonsense farmer who had found the body and reported it to the police, were predictably precise factual descriptions of the location of the discovery. He had found the naked body a foot or a foot and a half from the mouth of the tunnel in water which was about twelve to fifteen inches deep. Under cross-examination, he further told the court that the feet of the child were pointing towards the tunnel, the child's head was completely submerged and that there was grass on both sides of the dyke, adding, after being recalled to the witness stand, that it was not a fast stream.

Interestingly, he recalled the presence of Mrs Dobney on his return to the scene of the crime, but provided no further information: 'Mrs Dobney came up at the time'. The lack of any reference to a conversation having taken place is frustrating, but also prompts a degree of incredulity and scepticism about the whole incident: the coincidence of Elizabeth Dobney just happening to turn up at a crucial moment of high drama was surprising, but then just silently walking away as if the discovery of a dead child in a drain was a commonplace of a morning walk from Langtoft to Market Deeping, is beyond belief.

The notes of the judge taken from the deposition of Inspector Thomas Pawson were equally matter of fact, thoroughly recorded in his official notebook at the time, it seems. The bridge where the body was found was located on the division drain; there was a separate drain in Langtoft just a hundred and fifty yards away, but they were separate drains; the level of the water when the child was found was two to three feet below the road; the sloping grassy banks were rather steep; the width across the banks was about three to four feet, and eighteen inches deep. There was some disagreement with the opinion of William Holmes concerning the strength of the current in that the Inspector thought it 'quite strong', running from right to left. The precision of his deposition confirmed that the Inspector had done his job, as did the additional note that on looking for footprints at the side of the drain he had discovered evidence of the grass having been trodden down and giving the impression that someone had slipped down the bank.

On cross-examination, the inspector offered the further information that the water in which William

Stanhope was found was eighteen inches deep and that the culvert was three foot square.

The notes written down by his Lordship relating to the arrest of Selina Stanhope in Derby reflected what had been reported in the newspapers, including her confession on the train back to Bourne.

An odd curiosity of Robert Lush's notes is that like the reporter for the *Lincolnshire Chronicle*, he had misheard the name of the bridge where Selina Stanhope was seen on the evening of 18th July: Nidd's Bridge was heard by the reporter as Nidge's Bridge and by his Lordship as Lidd's Bridge. Complaints about courtroom acoustics were not unfamiliar in the nineteenth-century.

The final notes taken at Nottingham were from the deposition of William Deacon who had performed the post mortem on the body of William Stanhope. The conclusions of the post mortem noted by the judge were the mundane stuff of the reports found in the newspapers. The condition of the lungs were consistent with drowning, but he conceded that the lungs would have been in a similar condition had the child been suffocated. However, the evidence of the stomach, containing small pieces of grass and mud, as well as water and milk, suggested that the child could not have been suffocated and later put into the water.

What was more interesting and certainly not

reported by either the *Lincolnshire Chronicle* or the *Stamford Mercury* were the surgeon's comments, made under cross-examination, which were responding to the Counsel for the Defence's proposed construction of alternative explanations for the death of the child, in particular, a supposed fatal attack of croup.

A sudden attack of spasmodic croup could result in death if not treated immediately. Such attacks were likely to come on during teething and William Stanhope had two teeth. However, William Deacon was sceptical about the possibility: 'Such a closing of the larynx is not very common'.

The notes suggest that Mr Kennedy continued to press the surgeon, as he was recalled for further cross-examination. The medical opinion, however, remained sceptical about the hypothesis of death by croup. Whilst conceding that such an attack 'would leave no post mortem sign', he doubted very much that it would occur in such a child and further, that the convulsions of croup could not cause death by suffocation.

It appears that William Deacon's only concessions to the Counsel for the Defence were that a drink of water might possibly contain the substances found in the stomach of the child and, surprisingly, that this was the only case of drowning which had come before him. Perhaps courtroom acoustics or the judge's hearing were to blame for such an improbable note.

In the final analysis, the extensive notes sent to the Home Office by Robert Lush were only a snapshot, which would have required a wider familiarity with the case to be fully understood, without supporting evidence. For that reason, the report of the trial judge containing analysis and reflection, rather than being a mere factual collection of accumulated depositions, would have been more useful as part of the decision-making process.

The report from Justice Lush outlined the key points of the case and whilst it lacked the directness of his thoughts on the fate of Emma Wade, a few months earlier, which 'entirely concurred' with the jury's recommendation for mercy, he certainly expressed no disagreement with either the plea for clemency nor the justification for that plea. The minuted note attached to the report which stated that 'effect might be given in this case to the recommendation of the jury and the sentence be commuted to penal servitude for life' suggests that the Home Office had tentatively made up its mind early on, based upon the report from the judge. The additional minute, requesting a meeting to be arranged between Richard Cross and Robert Lush concerning Selina Stanhope was in all probability a formality, rather than an urgent conversation: historically, the opinion of the trial judge was unlikely to be challenged by a Home Secretary, given his greater knowledge of the context of the crime and his experience of dealing with the minutiae of capital cases.

In addition to the report of the judge, the influence of face to face conversations with other powerful public figures, as opposed to the earnest written memorials and petitions, seems evident in the reprieve of Selina Stanhope. The letter published in the *Lincolnshire Chronicle* from Edward Chaplin MP makes it clear that like Sir John Dalrymple Hay in the earlier case of Emma Wade he had personal access to Richard Cross. Despite the claim that the Home Secretary did not consult with individuals in capital cases, it seems undeniable that he was willing to make time to speak with Honourable Members if pressed.

The final formal unfolding of the story of Selina Stanhope is recorded in an assortment of bureaucratic documents filed by the Home Office several years after she had been sentenced to penal servitude for life.

Some relate to mundane formalities administered by the Home Office and shared with the Directors of Convict Prisons, concerning the granting of discharge licences and terms of release from Woking prison to the Elizabeth Fry Refuge in Hackney, and finally, into domestic service on the edge of Central London.

The most interesting of the documents are two petitions begging a further commutation of sentence and their accompanying notes from Woking concerning the behaviour of Selina Stanhope in prison supporting the petitions.

The earliest of the two petitions, dated 7th July, 1887, was written by the Chaplain of Woking prison. It comprises of the usual stiff obsequious formulae associated with such documents, seeking to reassure the Home Secretary that should the prisoner be released she would live a truly repentant life, and further, that the Chaplain had been in contact with people who were willing to receive and support her on release.

The accompanying supporting notes to the petition, signed by William Clarke, record the conduct of Prisoner F147, Selina Stanhope, as having been 'fair'.

Whether it was due to the faint praise of Woking prison, the bland formality of the petition, or the fact that Selina Stanhope had only served seven years of a notional life sentence is not recorded, but the request was unsucessful. The Minutes initialled by four, possibly five different hands, on the document recording the receipt of the petition (Numbered 88782/15 and dated 9th July, 1887) do not explain the decision, but ominously note on 14th July, 'Nil at present'.

The clarity of the appeal process is somewhat muddied by what appears to be a muddled document bearing the name of Selina Stanhope, accompanied by the reference number 88782/16, but also containing information which seems to relate to a different prisoner. It bears a Home Office stamp dated 20th July, 1888, a stamp with the word 'Referred', dated 23rd December, and the stamp of the Directors of Convict Prisons, dated 26th December: all three contain numbers which do not seem to have any link to the case of Selina Stanhope. The Minutes, initialled by various hands, one dated 15th December and one 22nd December, seem to relate to Selina Stanhope, when they note, 'Will come up next November after 10 years' and 'Lay by till then', but are written beneath the reference A48622/2. The difficulty of disentangling the Kafkaesque document is compounded by it originally having been a printed sheet from Woking prison to be used for prisoners who had served ten years of their sentence, which the Home Office has partially masked by a pasted piece of paper in a clumsy attempt to repurpose it.

The second petition, dated 12th February, 1889, accompanied by endorsements from Woking which describe her conduct as 'good' and her industry as 'very good', was almost certainly written, possibly with support, by Selina Stanhope herself. The earlier petition of 1887 had been signed with her name, but the Home Office notes the identity of the petitioner as the acting Chaplain of the prison, and is confirmed by the precision of the language. The second petition, at times halting and consisting of one long sentence of nearly a hundred and fifty words, contrasts with that of the Chaplain. But what it lacks in fluency and formal correctness, it gains in authenticity; as an expression of the personal misfortunes of a woman who enjoyed few, if any advantages in life, it might have moved even the most aloof civil servant in the Home Office to the indiscretion of a tear.

Her reference to having completed 'more than nine weary years' in prison and to the 'hours of loneliness' reflecting on her situation are made all the more powerful by their flat factuality. In its artless declaration that she loved 'her Boy' and would 'sacrifice her own life to bring him back', it is difficult to resist the unwelcome conclusion that too many nineteenth-century women endured a life they would not have willingly chosen.

Selina Stanhope died childless.

Bibliography

Archives

National Archives, Kew

<u>Ref</u>:   HO   144/38/83399   (Reprieve   documents relating to Emma Wade)
HO   144/50/88782   (Reprieve   documents relating to Selina Stanhope)
MEPO 6/1 (Register of Habitual Criminals)
HO   24/14   (Millbank   Register   of   Female Prisoners 1865-1874)

Lincolnshire Archives, Lincoln

Bourne   Workhouse   Register   of   Admissions   and Discharges, 1876-1880
<u>Ref</u>: PL/2/302/10

HMP Nominal Record, February 1878 - November, 1879, p.137 (Emma Wade) and p.164 (Selina Stanhope)
Ref: 2 LINCOLN PRISON/1

Prison Journal of James Foster, Governor
Ref: CoC 5/1//5/6: 1860-1868

Prison Journal of the Reverend Henry W Richter, Chaplain
Ref: CoC 5/1/21: 1839-1845
    CoC 5/1/22: 1845-1850
    CoC 5/1/27: 1866-1878

Sussex Archives, Ipswich

Diaries of George Gathorne Hardy, , Home Secretary, later Lord Cranbrook, 1866-1892
Ref: HA43:T501/294

Directories

Kelly, E R, *Directory of Lincolnshire with the Port of Hull and Neighbourhood with Map of the County*, various dates

White, William, *History, Gazetteer, and the Directory of Lincolnshire and the City and Diocese of Lincoln*, various dates

Wright, C.N., *Commercial and General Directory, Gazetteer, and Blue Book of Nottinghamshire*, (Barker & Co: Leicester: 9th edition, 1879)

Census records
1841-1891

Newspapers

Lucy Ann Buxton

Lincolnshire Chronicle, 10th January, 1851, p.3

Stamford Mercury, 10th January, 1851, p.4

Stamford Mercury, 14th April, 1854, p.3

Lincolnshire Chronicle, 28th September, 1867, p.5

Lincolnshire Chronicle, 4th October, 1867, p.5

Lincolnshire Chronicle, 18th October, 1867, p.7

Stamford Mercury, 18th October, 1867, p.6

Lincolnshire Chronicle, 1st May, 1868, p.5

Stamford Mercury, 1st May, 1868, p.5

Lincolnshire Chronicle, 8th May, 1868, p.5

Lincolnshire Chronicle, 15th May, 1868, p.8

Stamford Mercury, 15th May, 1868, p.5

Sleaford Gazette, 16th May, 1868, p.1

The Times, 27th July, 1868, p.11

Newark Advertiser, 29th July, 1868, p.7

Western Daily Press, 29th July, 1868, p.3

Hull and Eastern Counties Herald, 30th July, 1868, p.3

Lincolnshire Chronicle, 31st July, 1868, p.5

Nottingham Guardian, 31st July, 1868, p.11

Stamford Mercury, 31st July, 1868, p.3

Lincolnshire Chronicle, 1st August, 1868, p.6

Stamford Mercury, 7th August, 1868, p.4

Grantham Journal, 8th August, 1868, p.3

Sleaford Gazette, 8th August, 1868, p.4

Stamford Mercury, 28th August, 1868, p.4

Lincolnshire Chronicle, 10th October, 1868, p.4

Stamford Mercury, 16th October, 1868, p.4

Lincolnshire Chronicle, 9th January, 1869, p.6

Emma Wade

Stamford Mercury, 25TH April, 1879, p.4

Sleaford Gazette, 26TH April, 1879, p.4

Nottingham Evening Post, 29th April, 1879, p.2

Leeds Mercury, 1st May, 1879, p.3

Leicester Daily Mercury, 1st May, 1879, p.4

Manchester Evening News, 1st May, p.4

Nottingham Evening Post, 1st May, 1879, p.4

Nottingham Journal, 1st May, 1879, p.3

Pall Mall Gazette, 1st May, 1879, p.10

Sheffield Independent, 1st May, 1879, p.2

The Globe, 1st May, 1879, p.2

Yorkshire Post and Leeds Intelligencer, 1st May, 1879, p.5

Lincolnshire Chronicle, 2ND May, 1879, p.6

Stamford Mercury, 2nd May, 1879, pp.4 and 6

Boston Guardian, 2nd May, 1879, p.2

Leeds Mercury, 2nd May, 1879, p.4

Grantham Journal, 3rd May, 1879, p.3

Market Rasen Mail and Lincoln Advertiser, 3rd May, 1879, p.5

Daily Telegraph and Courier, 5th May, 1879, p.2

Manchester Evening News, 8th May, 1879, p.4

Sheffield Independent, 8th May, 1879, p.5

Soulby's Ulverston Advertiser and General Intelligencer, 8th May, 1879, p.3

Lincolnshire Chronicle, 9th May, 1879, p.5

Nottingham Journal, 9th May, 1879, p.3

Stamford Mercury, 9th May, 1879, pp.4, 5 and 6

Grantham Journal, 10th May, 1879, p.2

Market Rasen Weekly Mail and Lincoln Advertiser, 10th May, 1879, p.2

Peterborough and Huntingdonshire Standard, 10th May, 1879, pp.4 and 8

Sheffield Independent, 10th May, 1879, p.10

Sleaford Gazette, 10th May, p.4

The Examiner, 10th May, 1879, pp.605-606

Wakefield Free Press, 10th May, 1879, p.3

York Herald, 10th May, 1879, p.5

Grantham Journal, 24th May, 1879, p.4

Sheffield Daily Telegraph, 26th May, 1879, p.2

Stamford Mercury, 30th May, 1879, pp.2 and 5

Selina Stanhope

Stamford Mercury, 25th July, 1879, p.4

Grantham Journal, 26th July, 1879, p.2

Lincolnshire Chronicle, 28th July, 1879, p.5

Lincolnshire Chronicle, 1st August, 1879, p.6

Stamford Mercury, 1st August, 1879, p.5

Derbyshire Times, 2nd August, 1879, p.5

Grantham Journal, 2nd August, 1879, p.2

Derby Daily Telegraph, 11th November, 1879, pp.2 and 3

Lincolnshire Chronicle, 14th November, 1879, p.3

Stamford Mercury, 14th November, 1879, p.3

Daily News, 20th November, 1879, p.3

Derby Daily Telegraph, 20th November, p.2

Boston Guardian, 21st November, 1879, p.2

Lincolnshire Chronicle, 21st November, 1879, p.5

Nottinghamshire Evening Post, 21st November, 1879, p.2

Stamford Mercury, 21st November, 1879, p.4

Bradford Observer, 22nd November, 1879, p.5

Grantham Journal, 22nd November, 1879, p.2

Manchester Evening News, 22nd November, 1879, p.3

Newark Herald, 22nd November, 1879, p.4

The News of the World, 23rd November, 1879, p?

Lincolnshire Chronicle, 28th November, 1879, p.5

Nottingham Evening Post, 28th November, 1879, p.3

Stamford Mercury, 28th November, 1879, p.5

Grantham Journal, 29th November, 1879, p.2

Nottinghamshire Guardian, 5th December, 1879, p.6

Selected Books

The Capital Punishment Commission; together with

Home Office v *Town Talk*, in Albert D Pionke and Denise Tischler Millstein (ed), *Victorian Secrecy: Economies of Knowledge and Concealment*, (Ashgate Publishing Limited: Farnham, 2010), pp.179-192

Internet Articles

Richard Platt, *History of Langtoft*, https://langtoft. parish.lincolnshire.gov.uk/parish-information/ history-langtoft-1/1